How Brands Grow

Dedication

This book is dedicated to Professors Andrew Ehrenberg
and Gerald Goodhardt who collaboratively worked to
establish many of marketing's first scientific laws.

The building block of science is empirical generalization.
(Frank Bass, 1993)

*Even in a field supposed to be dominated by people's impulses
to buy—that of marketing—there are striking regularities ...
[yet] people seldom expect there to be law-like regularities in
social science ('Is it a science?'), and therefore do not even look
for them.* (Andrew Ehrenberg, 1993)

---

how brands grow

what marketers don't know

Byron Sharp and the
researchers of the
Ehrenberg-Bass Institute

OXFORD

UNIVERSITY PRESS

AUSTRALIA & NEW ZEALAND

OXFORD
UNIVERSITY PRESS

Oxford University Press is a department of the University of Oxford.
It furthers the University's objective of excellence in research,
scholarship, and education by publishing worldwide. Oxford is a registered
trademark of Oxford University Press in the UK and in certain other
countries.

Published in Australia by
Oxford University Press
253 Normanby Road, South Melbourne, Victoria 3205, Australia

First published 2010
Reprinted 2010, 2011, 2012, 2013, 2014, 2015, 2016, 2017, 2018, 2019, 2020

National Library of Australia Cataloguing-in-Publication data

Sharp, Byron.
How brands grow: what marketers don't know / Byron Sharp.

ISBN 978 0 19 557356 5 (pbk)

Bibliography.

Marketing.
Branding (Marketing)
Brand name products—Management.

658.83

Text design and typeset by Cannon Typesetting
Proofread by Bruce Gillespie
Printed in Hong Kong by Sheck Wah Tong Printing Press Ltd

# Contents

List of Laws

The law-like patterns (empirical generalisations) that are introduced in this book are:

- **Double jeopardy law:** Brands with less market share have far fewer buyers, and these buyers are slightly less loyal (in their buying and attitudes). See Chapter 2.
- **Retention double jeopardy:** All brands lose some buyers; this loss is proportionate to their market share (i.e. big brands lose more customers; though these represent a smaller proportion of their total customer base). See Chapter 3.
- **Pareto law: 60/20:** Slightly more than half a brand's sales come from the top 20% of its customers. The remaining sales come from the bottom 80% of its customers (i.e. the Pareto law is not 80/20). See Chapter 4.
- **Law of buyer moderation:** In subsequent time periods heavy buyers buy less often than in the base period that was used to categorise them as heavy buyers. Also, light buyers buy more often and some non-buyers become buyers. This 'regression to the mean' phenomenon occurs even when there has been no real change in buyer behaviour. See Chapter 4.
- **Natural monopoly law:** Brands with more market share attract a greater proportion of light category buyers. See Chapter 7.
- **User bases seldom vary:** Rival brands sell to very similar customer bases. See Chapter 5.

- **Attitudes and brand beliefs reflect behavioural loyalty:**
Consumers know and say more about brands they use, and
think and say little about brands they do not use. Therefore,
larger brands always score higher on surveys that assess attitudes
to brands because they have more users (who are also slightly
more loyal).

- **Usage drives attitude (or I love my Mum and you love yours):**
Buyers of different brands express very similar attitudes and
perceptions about their respective brands. See Chapter 5.

- **Law of prototypicality:** Image attributes that describe the product
category score higher (i.e. are more commonly associated with a
brand) than less prototypical attributes. See Chapter 8.

- **Duplication of purchase law:** A brand's customer base overlaps
with rival brands in line with its market share (i.e. in a time period
a brand will share more of its customers with large brands and
fewer with small brands). If 30% of a brand's buyers also bought
brand A in a period, then 30% of every rival brand's customers
also bought brand A. See Chapter 6.

- **NBD-Dirichlet:** A mathematical model of how buyers vary in
their purchase propensities (i.e. how often they buy the category
and which brands they buy). It correctly describes and explains
many of the above laws. The Dirichlet is one of marketing's few
true scientific theories. For more technical information on this
mathematical model (and related software) visit the Ehrenberg-
Bass Institute's website <www.MarketingScience.info>.

Contributors

Byron Sharp

Professor Byron Sharp is the Director of the Ehrenberg-Bass Institute for Marketing Science at the University of South Australia. The institute's research is used and financially supported by many of the world's leading corporations, including Coca-Cola, Kraft, Kellogg's, British Airways, Procter & Gamble, Nielsen, TNS, Turner Broadcasting, Network Ten, Simplot and Mars.

Byron has published over 100 academic papers and is on the editorial board of five journals. He recently co-hosted a conference at the Wharton Business School on the laws of advertising, and with Professor Jerry Wind he edited the 2009 special issue of the *Journal of Advertising Research* on laws of advertising. For more information about Byron, visit his website <www.byronsharp.com>.

John Dawes

Dr John Dawes is Associate Professor at the Ehrenberg-Bass Institute for Marketing Science, University of South Australia. John has an extensive background in sales and marketing prior to becoming an academic researcher. He has published in journals such as the *Journal of Services Research*, *Wall Street Journal*, *International Journal of Market Research*, and the *Journal of Brand Management*.

John is the editor of the *Journal of Empirical Generalisations in Marketing Science* (EMPGENS) <www.empgens.com>.

Jenni Romaniuk

Dr Jenni Romaniuk is Associate Research Professor at the Ehrenberg-Bass Institute.

Jenni's research covers brand salience, brand image tracking, how to use advertising to build brands, brand positioning, customer defection, and how to understand and use the brand perception–behaviour link.

Jenni has published in journals such as the *Journal of Marketing Management, Marketing Theory, European Journal of Marketing, International Journal of Market Research, Journal of Advertising Research* and the *Journal of Financial Services Marketing*. For the past eight years she has been providing advice on brand development strategies to companies in industries as diverse as retail, food, tourism, financial services, insurance, telecommunications, universities, event management and government departments.

John Scriven

John Scriven is Director of the Ehrenberg Centre at London South Bank University. The Ehrenberg Centre works in partnership with the Ehrenberg-Bass Institute to run the Corporate Sponsor Program. This is a special program of research into marketing that is supported by companies across the globe including Coca-Cola, Kraft, Kellogg's, British Airways, Procter & Gamble, Nielsen, TNS, Turner Broadcasting, Network Ten, Simplot and Mars.

John specialises in the study of brand performance measures and the effects of marketing inputs, particularly price and advertising. He has over 20 years experience in marketing, market research and marketing planning; he has held marketing positions with three major corporations: United Biscuits, RJR/Nabisco and Pepsico.

Preface

Marketing is a creative profession. So is architecture: architects design masterpieces like the Taj Mahal and the Sydney Opera House, but architects use their creativity within a framework of physical laws. Architects must design buildings that will not collapse under their own weight or blow over in a breeze; they cannot choose to ignore the law of gravity, or hope their building is immune to the laws of physics.

Marketers, even senior marketing academics, like to say that there can be no laws concerned with marketing. These people argue that consumers are far too individual and unpredictable.[1] Research has shown this is utter nonsense. This ill-founded belief stops academics doing their job and searching for law-like patterns in buying behaviour and marketing effects. It also allows marketers to carry on with 'anything goes' marketing plans. Imagine if architects designed 'anything goes' plans ('Let's build out of fairy-floss!', 'Let's add another 68 floors!')

Marketers argue with each other about things that have nothing to do with the creativity of the discipline; about things that should be known for certain. It's time for this to stop. This book reveals the predictable patterns in how buyers buy, and how sales grow—things all marketers should know, not argue about.

---

1   It is a common mistake to associate the concept of randomness with unpredictability, yet as any casino owner knows, random events lead to great predictability. A casino cannot predict who will win what, but they can predict with pin-point accuracy how many wins and loses there will be overall (and so how much money the casino will make).

These patterns are valuable knowledge. It's often thought that great marketing strategy is obvious—with hindsight everyone can see what you did and copy you. This might be true for new products or some advertising campaigns, but in reality marketing offers the ability to outperform competitors while they scratch their heads wondering why on earth you are doing so well. Unfortunately, marketers themselves often have no idea why one of their own campaigns worked and others did not. Their explanations as to what they got right or wrong are often wide of the mark because their assumptions (the theories in their head) are wrong.

This book is for marketers who are willing to learn new things based on classical science, and to shake off the superstition (and unfounded speculation) that today passes for marketing theory.

Read the assumptions in Table 1 below.

Table 1: Marketing assumptions

Strategic assumptions	True, false, or don't know?
Differentiating our brand is a vital marketing task.	
Loyalty metrics reflect the strength, not size, of our brand.	
Customer retention is cheaper than acquisition.	
Price promotions boost penetration not loyalty.	
Who we compete with depends on the positioning of our brand image.	
Mass marketing is dead and no longer competitive.	
Buyers have a special reason to buy our brand.	
Our consumers are a distinctive type of person.	
20% of our heaviest customers deliver at least 80% of our sales.	

If you believe that most of these are true, you are operating under many false assumptions. This book will give you the evidence. If it changes your mind it might revolutionise your marketing.

Table 2: Towards a new view of marketing priorities

Past world model	Positioning	Differentiation	Message comprehension	Unique selling propositions	Persuasion	Teaching	Rational involved viewers
New world model	Salience	Distinctiveness	Getting noticed, emotional response	Relevant associations	Refreshing and building memory structures	Reaching	Emotional distracted viewers

The most important knowledge contained in this book

Decades of research into how buyers buy and how brands compete has led to these surprising conclusions:

1   Growth in market share comes by increasing popularity; that is, by gaining many more buyers (of all types), most of whom are light customers buying the brand only occasionally.
2   Brands, even though they are usually slightly differentiated, mainly compete as if they are near lookalikes; but they vary in popularity (and hence market share).
3   Brand competition and growth is largely about building two market-based assets: physical availability and mental availability. Brands that are easier to buy—for more people, in more situations— have more market share. Innovation and differentiation (when they work) build market-based assets, which last after competitors copy the innovation.

Therefore, marketers need to improve the branding of their product (i.e. it needs to stand out) and to continuously reach large audiences of light buyers cost effectively. Marketers need to know what their distinctive brand assets are (colours, logos, tone, fonts, etc.); they need to use and protect these. They also need to know how buyers buy their brand, when they think of and notice it, and how it fits into their lives. They need to manage media and distribution in line with these facts.

Advertising works largely by refreshing, and occasionally building, memory structures. Marketers need to research these memory structures and ensure that their advertising refreshes these structures by consistently using the brand's distinctive assets.

In short, there is a great deal to learn, and much to be discovered, about sophisticated mass marketing.

Tables 3, 4 and 5 below summarise old and new attitudes to different aspects of marketing.

Table 3: Consumer behaviour

Past world view	Attitude drives behaviour	Brand loyals	Brand switchers	Deeply committed buyers	Involvement	Rational, involved viewers
New world view	Behaviour drives attitude	Loyal switchers	Loyal switchers	Uncaring cognitive misers	Heuristics	Emotional, distracted viewers

Table 4: Brand performance

Past world view	Growth through targeting brand loyals	Unpredictable, confusing brand metrics	Price promotions win new customers	Target marketing	We compete on positioning	Differentiation
New world view	Growth through penetration	Predictable meaningful brand metrics	Price promotions reach existing loyal customers	Sophisticated mass marketing	We compete with all brands in the category	Distinctiveness

Table 5: Advertising

Past world view	Positioning	Message comprehension	Unique selling propositions	Persuasion	Teaching	Campaign bursts
New world view	Salience	Getting noticed, emotional response	Relevant associations	Refreshing and building memory structures	Reaching	Continuous presence

Examples in this book

The scientific laws presented in this book apply to many categories:

- products and services
- industrial products and supermarket packaged goods
- national and retailer brands
- brand buying and store choice.

The laws apply across countries and have held for decades. This is why they can provide useful predictions.

I've tried to demonstrate the breadth of generalisation by deliberately using diverse examples; for example, retention levels for cars in France and banks in Australia. I am grateful to Nielsen and TNS for providing data spanning many countries. Please don't infer that just because the example refers to, say, UK store brands, that the law doesn't apply to your category. If you are in doubt, please refer to the cited references, as these will provide further examples that illustrate the breadth of the law.

Acknowledgments

The laws in this book might not been discovered without the years of research that has been funded by corporations around the world. I thank the following corporations for their many years of continuing support:

- ABC
- ANZ National Financial Group
- AOL (UK)
- Australian Central Credit Union
- Australian Research Council
- Bank of New Zealand
- BankSA
- BASES
- Bayer Consumer Care
- Boots Healthcare
- Boral
- BP
- Bristol-Myers Squibb
- British Airways
- BT
- Cadbury
- Caxton Publishers & Printers
- CBS
- Channel 4
- Clemenger BBDO
- Coca-Cola
- Colgate-Palmolive
- Commonwealth Bank of Australia
- ConAgra Foods
- Dairy Farmers
- SA Department for Environment and Heritage
- DDB Worldwide Communications Group
- Diageo
- Distell
- Dulux
- dunnhumby
- Elders
- ESPN
- FirstRand
- Fonterra Brands
- Foster's Wine Estates
- General Mills
- General Motors
- Goodman Fielder
- Hamilton Laboratories
- Hills Industries

- Insurance Australia Group
- IPC Magazines
- ITV
- J Walter Thompson
- Kellogg's
- Kraft
- Leo Burnett
- London South Bank University
- Marks & Spencer
- Mars Inc
- Meat & Livestock Australia
- Mediaedge:cia
- Media Trust
- Millward Brown
- Molson
- Mountainview Learning
- MTV
- National Pharmacies
- Network Ten
- News International
- Ogilvy & Mather
- Origin Energy
- PepsiCo
- Pfizer Consumer Healthcare
- Procter & Gamble
- PZ Cussons
- Reckitt Benckiser
- Research International
- Roy Morgan Research
- SABMiller
- St.George Bank
- S.C. Johnson
- Selleys
- Simplot Australia
- South Australian R&D Institute
- South Australian Tourism Commission
- Standard Life
- TD Canada Trust
- The Edrington Group
- The Queen Elizabeth Hospital Research Foundation
- The Nielsen Company
- The Walt Disney Company
- TNS
- Tourism Australia
- Tourism New Zealand
- Turner Broadcasting
- TVNZ
- Unilever
- University of South Australia
- Wm. Wrigley Jr. Company
- Wyeth Consumer Healthcare
- Young & Rubicam

Special thanks

I would like to especially thank my gifted and hard working colleagues in the Ehrenberg-Bass Institute, University of South Australia, and the Ehrenberg Centre at London SouthBank University. Special thanks also to Dr Thomas Bayne at Mountainview Learning for working with me to show marketing executives around the world how scientific discoveries can revolutionise their strategies.

Evidence-based Marketing

Byron Sharp

I magine you are the Insights Director of Colgate Palmolive. Margaret, the Senior Category Manager for toothpaste, is standing at your office door and she is obviously distressed. She is waving a recently received report from your global market research supplier, and this is what it shows:[1]

Figure 1.1: Toothpaste brands: US market shares

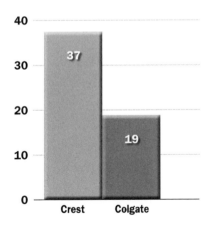

Source: Spaeth & Hess, 1989.

---

1   This is real data from a Chicago single-source panel reported in Spaeth & Hess (1989).

The market research shows that Procter & Gamble's Crest toothpaste has double the market share of Colgate in the US. However, this has long been known and is not the reason why Margaret is upset. It's the next couple of graphs that have her worried (see Figures 1.2 and 1.3).

Figure 1.2: Crest consumer base

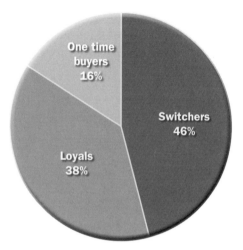

Source: Spaeth & Hess, 1989.

Figure 1.3: Colgate consumer base

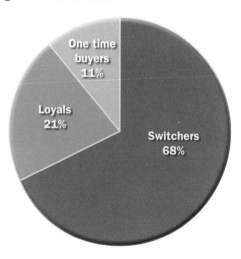

Source: Spaeth & Hess, 1989.

They decompose the sales volume of each rival brand according to the recent repeat-buying behaviour of their consumers.

The percentage of Colgate's sales that came from loyal customers is almost half that of Crest's 'loyals' sales, 'loyals' being people who bought the brand for the majority of their toothpaste purchasing during the analysis period. Colgate's sales come much more from 'switchers'—people who bought Colgate at least once in the analysis period, although most of their buying was of other brands.

Margaret is demanding an explanation. What does this mean? Why is Colgate's sales base so unhealthy? Is the brand doomed? What does this mean for her ambitious growth targets?

How would you answer?

Of course, you would call for more research. It's an Insight Director's prerogative.

The additional research breaks down the market share of each company further by analysing the switchers within both the Crest and Colgate customer bases.

The additional research consists of a survey; the first question of which asks customers about their attitudinal loyalty. Figure 1.4 reports the percentage of switchers who agree with the statement, 'This is my preferred brand.' (The switcher group is the interesting one, as we can safely assume that both Crest's and Colgate's loyals will report that their brand is their preferred one.)

As you can see, Figure 1.4 shows that Crest switchers are substantially more likely to say that Crest is their preferred brand.

The survey's second question asks customers about their perceptions of quality. Figure 1.5 reports the quality perceptions of the switchers in each customer base.

Both Crest and Colgate buyers perceive both brands to be quality products—as they should, because these are both well researched and well-made products. People who buy Colgate (who also often buy other brands) are slightly more likely to state that Colgate is a quality brand than Crest.

Figure 1.4: Percentage of brand buyers who say, 'This is my preferred brand'

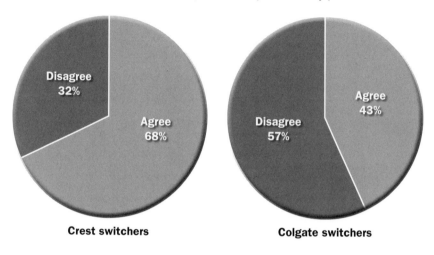

Source: Spaeth & Hess, 1989.

Figure 1.5: Percentage of brand buyers who say, 'This is a quality product'

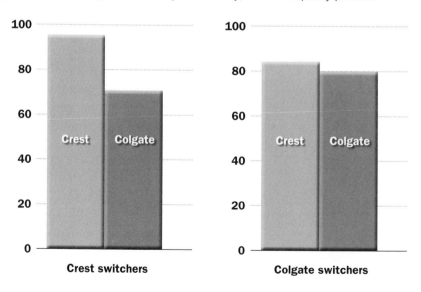

Source: Spaeth & Hess, 1989.

Here are the 'brand insights' the market research agency reports:

- Colgate's sales volume comes mostly from non-loyal buyers
- Colgate is 50% more dependent on switchers than Crest
- Colgate buyers are less loyal, both behaviourally and attitudinally
- Even Colgate buyers think Crest is a quality product
- Colgate is a quality product but it has perception problems and lacks loyalty
- Colgate is attracting the wrong sort of buyer.

These insights are translated into the following **action recommendations**. Colgate needs:

- more persuasive advertising that stresses Colgate's quality
- comparative advertisements against Crest
- media schedules that emphasise frequency of exposure (to shift attitudes)
- research to profile Colgate 'loyals' with the aim of attracting more people like this.

All this sounds perfectly normal. It happens in marketing departments around the world every day. You personally may have come up with a somewhat different marketing strategy, depending on your own experience, preferences, or creativity, but the insights and the strategy appear reasonable, and not unusual. *Except that they are wrong.*

The 'insights' suggested here reflect ignorance of relevant scientific laws about buyer behaviour and marketing metrics, laws that we'll cover in this book.

Consequently, Colgate's fictional Insights Director is jumping at shadows, and overly worrying Margaret. Colgate's loyalty metrics, both attitudinal and behavioural, are normal for a brand with half the market share of Crest. Indeed all the other research findings are essentially repeating the findings of the first graph (Figure 1.1), that is, that Colgate is half the size of Crest in this market. These metrics don't show why it is half the size; they are what they are *because* of Colgate's size. All will be explained in the forthcoming chapters (if you can't wait, turn to page vii for an explanation of the laws that relate to this Colgate case study).

Are marketers bleeding the companies that employ them?

I am in awe of the modern market economy and the diversity and quality of products it delivers. This modern economy is the product of one of the most incredible social experiments: in the twentieth century classical, planned economies were tried alongside more market economies (Hunt & Morgan, 1995). The results were startling. Market economies won by a mile, as they provide people with more choice, fewer queues, and better, cheaper products and services. For example, within a few hundred metres of where I am sitting I have a choice of multiple grocery stores, bakeries, pharmacies, cafes, wine stores, even several fine chocolate shops. Not bad!

When I was in Thailand my charming host Professor Tasman Smith asked if we had many Thai restaurants back home in Adelaide, Australia. I did a quick mental count and replied, 'Yes, there are six within a short walk from our house.' This illustrates the fact that those who live in developed market economies are spoilt for choice—we can eat pizza in Thailand, or order a curry in Paris, if we want to. This is because today's marketers do a good job of getting attractive goods to market.

But marketing is far from perfect; there is much waste. This matters because marketing activities consume a vast amount of our time—as Robert Louis Stevenson said, 'Everybody lives by selling something.' Poor marketing wastes an incalculable amount of resources, and it prevents and slows the uptake of life-enhancing products and social initiatives.

Marketing practice, for all its advances, has never been strong on evaluation; there is plenty of ineffectiveness and room for improvement. Response rates to advertising are a good example of marketing inefficiency. However you define a consumer response—from clicking on a web ad to driving to a store—response levels are extremely low and falling. It's even more scary if you look at the impact of advertising on memory. For example, one of our yet-to-be-published studies on advertising productivity examined 143 ads on Australian television that were screened on consecutive weeknight evenings. That weekend respondents were telephoned and those who watched the programs during which the ads were played were asked if they recognised the particular television commercial (i.e. each ad was verbally described to only those people who had an opportunity to see it). The average recognition score for a television ad was barely 40% (i.e. 40% of potential viewers noticed the ad when it aired). Those respondents who recognised the ad were then asked what brand it was for, and on average the correct brand was linked to only approximately 40% of the ads. Consider that for an ad to work it needs to at the very least be noticed, processed *and* be linked to the correct brand. So only around 16%[2] of these advertising exposures passed the two necessary hurdles; put another way, there was 84% wastage!

Note that the ads' effectiveness varied widely. Some were noticed by more viewers, and correctly branded too. But most were not. This suggests that there is much to gain from learning how to make better advertising.

There is much to learn about marketing. Even educated and very senior marketers believe many things that are wrong, and there are many important facts that simply aren't widely known. Many well-paid marketers are operating with wrong assumptions, so they are making mistakes, and wasting money, without even knowing it.

Marketing professionals today are better educated than in the past, and they have access to much more data on buying behaviour. But the study of marketing is so young that we would be arrogant to believe that we know it all, or even that we have got the basics right yet. We can draw an analogy with medical practice. For centuries this noble profession has attracted some of the best and brightest people in society, who were typically far better educated than other professionals. Yet for 2500 years these experts enthusiastically and universally taught and practised bloodletting

---

2   Near identical results are reported 15 years ago in du Plessis (1994). A figure around 16% is also not uncommon in advertising recall (i.e. where the brand name is the cue for recalling the ad).

(a generally useless and often fatal 'cure'). Only very recently, about 80 years ago, medical professionals started doing the very opposite, and today blood transfusions save numerous lives every day. Marketing managers operate a bit like Medieval doctors—working on impressions and myth-based explanations.

It would be arrogant to think that the current marketing 'best practice' does not contain many mistakes and erroneous assumptions. I used to teach some erroneous stuff to my university students; I know how easy it is to parrot nonsense simply because that's what we were taught to think and it appears to make sense. This book challenges some of the conventional wisdom with empirical evidence. I hope you find this 'myth-busting' knowledge as liberating as it is useful.

Marketing texts

Marketing prides itself on being a practical discipline, so marketing texts (textbooks, marketing magazines, consultant reports, etc.) should be full of answers to practical questions, such as:

- What will happen to sales if I change the price of the product?
- Why can I see the effect of price promotions in the sales data, but the advertising campaigns barely show up, if at all? Is advertising not generating sales?
- What is a reasonable cross-selling target?
- Will the new brand cannibalise sales from the current brand? If so, by how much?
- Should I pay double for a full-page newspaper ad or buy the half-page ad instead?
- When should 15-second television ads be used?

Yet it is difficult to find answers to such practical questions, let alone to find explanatory and predictive theories that can be used to provide the solutions.

A good colleague of mine, Scott Armstrong, Professor at the Wharton School, once put marketing principles texts to the test (Armstrong &

Schultz, 1992, pp. 253–65). He asked four doctoral students to independently go through nine leading texts looking for managerial principles. They found many (566) normative ('you should do') statements, but the texts failed to accompany the statements with supporting empirical evidence. The students only found twenty statements that were clear and meaningful. When these twenty statements were sent to marketing professors they rated only half as true, and said they knew of supporting evidence for only two. Only one single statement was universally rated as true, supported by evidence, as well as being considered managerially useful—but this principle was also rated as 'unsurprising, even to someone who had never taken a marketing course'.[3]

We could dismiss our texts as harmless introductions to marketing practice, but marketing texts aren't harmless, because they routinely lead managers astray. Texts tell us what to worry about (customer satisfaction, image perceptions, brand equity, loyalty), what we should be doing (segmentation, targeting), what techniques to use, and what metrics to measure. Marketing texts largely reflect and reinforce current practice and existing beliefs. They contain a lot of good basic information, like telling us that if we want to advertise we should remember to book the media. But texts are also full of myths; the sort of myths that sap the effectiveness and productivity of marketing departments.

Many of the things that marketing people think are important, such as loyalty programs, aren't (see Chapter 11). Many of the 'facts' marketing people believe, particularly about brand buying, are incorrect. Furthermore, many marketers lack the deep knowledge necessary to ask the questions that will lead to new valuable insights.

Take the following test on strategic assumptions (Table 1.1). Marketing professionals agree that these assumptions really matter; they underpin strategic marketing decisions that are linked to substantial expenditure. How would you and your marketing colleagues answer these questions?

---

3   The statement said that in conducting advertising experiments, test cities should be isolated so that promotions in one city don't influence sales in another.

Would there be consensus? If your answers were questioned, could you point to anything more than anecdotes to support your view?

Table 1.1: Strategic assumptions test

Strategic assumptions	True, false, or don't know?
Differentiating our brand is a vital marketing task.	
Loyalty metrics reflect the strength, not size, of our brand.	
Retention is cheaper than acquisition.	
Price promotions boost penetration not loyalty.	
Who we compete with depends on the positioning of our brand image.	
Mass marketing is dead or, at the very least, no longer competitive.	
Buyers have a special reason why they buy our brand.	
Our buyers are a distinctive type of person.	
20% of our buyers deliver at least 80% of our sales.	

If you answer true to most of the questions above then you are operating under false assumptions. This book will give you the evidence. As Mark Twain wrote in his notebook in 1898, 'Education consists mainly of what we have unlearned.'

False assumptions have led us astray in the past

Science's systematic approach to discovery is a relatively recent practice that didn't really get going until around the 1700s. Prior to that, knowledge largely came from myth, folk-tale, and from experts in authority (chiefs, priests, kings and queens). How these 'experts' acquired their knowledge no-one knew or dared ask. Most of the time their understanding was wrong, and there were glaring gaps. This lack of accurate knowledge meant we didn't think to ask useful questions. So for millions of years humans made little progress; life was typically short, painful and we were hungry and cold much of the time. In the past few hundred years we've made extraordinary progress. Our combined knowledge has grown in leaps and bounds, and we live in comparative luxury.

Let's return for a moment to the case of our learned but bloodletting doctors. For centuries they bled patients for almost every possible ailment, indeed many advocated bleeding simply to maintain good health. For most of the last millennium bloodletting was as trusted and popular in Europe as aspirin is today (Starr, 1998).[4] Over the years, doctors must have killed hundreds of thousands of patients. Among them was US President George Washington, who died when his doctors bled him vigorously to cure a sore throat. The doctor of another US legislator once wrote that he had treated his patient by relieving him of 165 ounces of blood in five days (almost all the blood in his body!). The doctor wrote, 'he died … had we taken a still greater quantity [of blood] the event might perhaps have been more fortunate' (Starr, 1998). Apart for a few rare medical conditions, bleeding does no good whatsoever. So how did these well-meaning and well-educated doctors get it so terribly wrong for so long?

First, it was because they believed untested theories that advocated bleeding. Like all practitioners they were, probably without realising it, deeply theoretical. The ancient Greeks (e.g. Hippocrates) developed a theory that all illness resulted from an imbalance of humours; bleeding and purging were common ways of addressing such imbalances. This humoural imbalance theory dominated medical thinking in Europe and the Middle East for 2000 years because no one tested if this really was the cause of illness.

Second, bleeding continued because no one conducted systematic research into its effects. If patients recovered from their illness then bleeding was credited as the cure, if they died … well they were sick after all!

---

4   Aspirin was not only one of the very first drugs to actually have proven affect, it
     was also the first to benefit from mass marketing. Every doctor in the UK was
     mailed information on the new drug which dramatically sped its adoption, much to
     the relief of early patients.

Doctors worked using their impressions, assumptions, commonsense, accepted wisdom, and scattered bits of data. This is very similar to the working practice of marketing managers today.

Adding to the danger, doctors overestimated how much blood was in the human body—no one checked properly. And they underestimated how long it would take the body to manufacture new blood—again no one checked.

Douglas Starr (1998) argues that bleeding was also popular because it gave doctors a sense of control. It produced dramatic results—patients fainted (for a long while this was considered a good thing). Patients demanded that doctors be seen to do something, and bleeding fulfilled this requirement. It's not hard to see similarities with many marketing interventions (like price promotions, bursts of advertising, and rushing into 'new media' like proverbial lemmings).[5]

The scientific revolution transformed medical practice as doctors, and statisticians such as Florence Nightingale, started compiling detailed records and case histories. The numbers they recorded started to generate insight into causes and effects, and germ theory eventually triumphed over humourial imbalance theory. Medical experiments gradually started separating the effectual from the ineffectual and the downright dangerous.

Today marketing managers operate a bit like nineteenth century doctors; they are affected by the scientific revolution, but are not yet governed by it. Even 'best practice' is still dominated by impressions and untested assumptions. Texts still contain untested, ungrounded theories and myths. And serious experimentation is rare.

The marketing equivalent of humourial imbalance theory may be the Kotlerian 'differentiate or die' world view where marketing success is entirely about creating superior products, selling these at a premium price, targeting the most likely buyers, and advertising to bring people's minds around to the product's superiority.

---

5   Actually, it is a myth that lemmings commit mass suicide.

You are reading a book about real-world facts and law-like relationships that challenge the fundamental tenets of modern marketing theory; the widespread beliefs that affect not just the *decisions* of marketing managers, but also how marketers *see* the world.

Commonplace marketing mistakes

Even the most intelligent marketers, in the best organisations, routinely make mistakes. Because many marketers operate using incorrect assumptions about how buyers buy and how marketing works, they emphasise the wrong things and ignore important points, consequently making mistakes such as:

- changing packaging in ways that confuse customers and reduce the brand's ability to be noticed
- creating advertising that doesn't build or refresh relevant memory structures
- failing to research what memory structures are devoted to the brand
- failing to research what makes the brand distinctive and noticeable
- creating advertising that isn't branded (other than a flash of the brand name)
- investing countless hours and many dollars on pointless tracking research that informs no decisions
- over-investing in already highly loyal consumers, while neglecting to reach new buyers
- pricing too high then trying to compensate with very regular price discounts
- teaching consumers to buy when the brand is discounted
- burning media dollars in advertising bursts then going silent for long periods (when consumers are still buying)
- paying premiums for low-reach media.

It's not that there is anything wrong with the intelligence of marketers, but like all professionals they need some empirically grounded guidance.

Law-like reoccurring patterns

The research that underpins this book is different from commercial market research because it focuses on finding fundamental patterns, not one-off events. These are findings that have a long use-by date because they have been found to hold for long periods of time, across all sorts of conditions (including across product and service categories, and countries). This research is also very different from most academic research, where each study is typically based on one single set of data, collected in one particular set of conditions, and so tells us almost nothing about the generalisability of the finding (where it holds and where it does not).[6]

Uncovering patterns that generalise is the fundamental work of science. It is only because we know that these scientific laws hold across a wide range of conditions that they can be used for prediction. And by knowing the many factors that do not affect the laws, and maybe the few that do, we gain deep explanatory insight into why things are the way they are, and how things work.

This is how science works.

Where do these discoveries come from?

This book draws largely from the work of researchers at the Ehrenberg-Bass Institute for Marketing Science. The early discoveries come from work started by Professor Andrew Ehrenberg and Professor Gerald Goodhardt five decades ago. Today this fundamental research continues at the Ehrenberg-Bass Institute at the University of South Australia, and the Ehrenberg Centre at London South Bank University. There are also plenty of like-minded researchers working inside and outside universities

---

6   It's a common mistake, made even by senior academics, to think that statistical significance tests tell us something about generalisability. They don't, and this isn't their purpose. They merely tell us something about the possibility that our result is really due to random sampling variation, that is, because we examined a small sample of the population not everyone. Statistical significance tests don't tell us which population our result might represent, or anything about the conditions where the result would vary.

around the world. These efforts receive encouragement and financial support from progressive corporations around the world including Turner Broadcasting, Mars, Colgate, Kraft, Procter & Gamble, General Motors, Network Ten, Mountain View Learning and many others. We are very grateful for this ongoing support.

Many of the findings in this book are emotionally confronting, because they clash with conventional wisdom. In order to make readers feel more psychologically comfortable with this 'myth busting' I have attempted to give a good feel for the empirical data[7] and how the analysis was done. I've done this by completely avoiding complicated obscuring statistics and algebra; there are no 'black box' (or 'trust me') techniques used, and references are supplied so that interested readers can delve further.

There is much potential for science to improve the effectiveness of marketing. The great advances in marketing that will be made this century won't be due to computers or sophisticated statistics. As in other professions, the real advances will come from the development and application of well established scientific laws (empirical generalisations). On behalf of my colleagues and co-authors I hope you find the new knowledge presented in this book exciting; I hope it also changes the way you see, and do, marketing.

---

7   All the tables in this book try to conform to Andrew Ehrenberg's principles of data reduction; see Ehrenberg (1998, 1999, 2000).

How Brands Grow

Byron Sharp

What is the secret key to growth? All the global market research agencies claim to provide an exclusive service that can tell if your brand is heading up or down. Every strategy consultancy says that only it can take you on the path to profitable share growth. Econometric modellers say they can quantify precisely which marketing mix will deliver maximum growth. This is all nonsense. If growth were that easy then all marketing directors would be out of a job, or paid a pittance of their current salary. No one can guarantee growth.

That said, this book does reveal a great deal about how brands grow. Marketing science has been chipping away at the problem for decades. There have already been some breakthroughs that every professional marketing person should know about.

The desire for growth

Have you ever met a marketer who was not interested in sales growth or, at the very least, interested in preventing losses? Growth is an ingrained part of our business culture. Marketing departments are expected to plan for and deliver growth. Marketing initiatives have to be justified in terms of growth potential. The main reason for this obsession with growth is the substantial fixed costs of most firms; this means that companies experience dramatic increases in profitability if they increase sales, and profits can be wiped out by comparatively small sales losses. So growth is very attractive.

However, market share growth is difficult. Markets are more competitive than ever. Marketers have to work very hard just to retain their current market share position; run very fast just to stand still. For example, the scope for price promotions to deliver any more growth is limited by the fact that we are running about as many promotions as the retail system can handle.

There is plenty to debate about whether an obsession with sales growth is good for profits in the long run, but let's accept the idea that it would be good to know more about how to deliver market share growth and prevent decline.

The difference between large and small brands

A sensible starting point in understanding growth is to compare competing brands that have different market shares. A million brands have attempted to grow—some have been successful and some not. Can we use these trillions of dollars worth of natural experiments to discover something universal about the differences between large and small brands? *Yes*; the difference between large and small brands, and growing and declining brands, is very revealing.

Again and again it appears in numerous product categories, markets and countries that there is a fundamental law of brand size:[1] big brands have markedly larger customer bases.

---

1   Much of this research was conducted by Andrew Ehrenberg and Gerald Goodhardt and associated colleagues from the 1960s onwards. It has also been verified by commercial analysts within large marketing firms such as Kraft, P&G and Unilever and the large research houses such as TNS and Nielsen. The law has also been recently independently rediscovered in an analysis of 10 000 brands in the US by researchers with no prior knowledge of the law (Hall & Stamp, 2004), and in an analysis of growing brands by Research International (presented by Jim Findlay in 2003 Advertising Research Foundation (ARF) 'Week of workshops').

This seems obvious—more sales equals more customers—yet it need not be this way. A brand's sales volume depends on two things:

1 how many buyers it has

2 how often they buy the brand.

One multiplied by the other equals sales. So a brand could be large because it is bought very often by its buyers, without having many buyers. Theoretically there could be two brands of equal size, one with many buyers who buy the brand occasionally, while the other brand has half the number of buyers but they buy it twice as often.[2] See Table 2.1 below for an illustration of this point.

Table 2.1: Different metrics that can result in equal sales volumes and shares

Hypothetical brands of equal size	Annual market penetration (%)	Number of theoretical purchases per buyer per annum	Resulting market share (%)
Dell-icious	32	3	14
AppleCore	16	6	14

But this happens only in theory, never in practice.[3] In the real world, two brands of about equal market share have around equal market penetration, and so they must also get bought by their buyers at a similar average rate.

2　An interesting question is which brand you would rather manage or own? The brand with the small but apparently very loyal customer base, or the brand with the larger customer base who buy it less often? The current fashion is for the former, with the argument being that it would be cheaper to service this smaller client base. But an equally compelling case can be made for the larger customer base being of greater strategic and financial value. Don't worry though, as all of this turns out to be academic. Reality (the double jeopardy law) renders this question pointless.

3　It's common to say that there are no absolutes in the social sciences but this is one: two rival brands of equal market share never have completely opposite penetration and loyalty metrics.

There is another related discovery: when you look at brands of markedly different sizes you typically see that their penetration metrics differ a lot,[4] while their average purchase rate varies little. Put another way: *loyalty doesn't vary much.*

This is not what fashionable marketing literature implies. We've all been taught that brands vary tremendously in loyalty, with brands like Apple held up as loyalty champions. We'll investigate Apple's loyalty levels further in Chapter 7 but for now let's just look at the discovery that loyalty metrics for competing brands are quite similar.

Loyalty doesn't vary much

If you look at marketing metrics (i.e. from consumer panels run by global market research agencies such as Nielsen and TNS) you'll see that the big brands have much higher penetrations and they also get bought slightly more often by their buyers—but not much more.

The following table (Table 2.2) deconstructs the market shares of major washing machine detergent brands. You can see that all brands are bought by their buyers slightly less often than four times a year. The largest brand, Persil, gets bought almost four times a year. Surf, the smallest, has fewer than half the number of buyers as Persil and these buyers buy Surf around three and a half times a year. This pattern is known as the 'double jeopardy' law because smaller brands get 'hit twice': their sales are lower because they have fewer buyers who buy the brand less often.

---

4   Penetration is a metric that records how many people bought the brand, at least once, in a particular time period. So any brand's penetration increases with time, but it doesn't double if you double the length of the time period because a lot of sales come from the same customers coming back and repeat buying. In many categories a brand's penetration fails to get anywhere near 100% even in a very long time period (e.g. years) because many buyers simply don't have the brand in their repertoire.

Table 2.2: Double jeopardy law—washing powder, UK 2005

Washing powder brands	Market share (%)	Annual market penetration (%)	Purchase frequency (average)
Persil	22	41	3.9
Ariel	14	26	3.9
Bold	10	19	3.8
Daz	9	17	3.7
Surf	8	17	3.4
Average			**3.7**

Note: Each brand's customers buy the brand at similar purchase rates.

Source: TNS.

The next table (Table 2.3) shows a slightly more glamorous category: shampoo. This table is interesting because both the market leader (P&G's Head & Shoulders) and the smallest brand (Wella's Vosene) are functionally different from the other brands—they are formulated to reduce dandruff. However, this does not substantively affect the double jeopardy law. All the brands get purchased about two times, with the market leaders being purchased slightly more often.

Table 2.3: Double jeopardy law—shampoo, UK 2005

Shampoo brands	Market share (%)	Annual market penetration (%)	Purchase frequency (average)
Head & Shoulders	11	13	2.3
Pantene	9	11	2.3
Herbal Essences	5	8	1.8
L'Oreal Elvive	5	8	1.9
Dove	5	9	1.6
Sunsilk	5	8	1.7
Vosene	2	3	1.7
Average			**1.9**

Note: Smaller UK shampoo brands suffer from only slightly lower loyalty.

Source: TNS.

In 2005, Head & Shoulders was bought by more than four times as many buyers as bought Vosene. This much larger customer base largely explains why Head & Shoulders had five times the sales of Vosene. Another small contributing factor is that buyers of Head & Shoulders were more loyal, buying it 0.6 times more often per annum.

Data from Nielsen shows that the US shampoo category exhibits the same pattern. Different brands, market shares, consumers, time period, consumer panel and analysts—but the same familiar double jeopardy pattern. Later we'll discuss why this occurs and what the loyalty implications are, but for now let's continue to focus on the implications of this scientific law for brand growth.

Table 2.4: Double jeopardy law—shampoo, US 2005

Shampoo brands	Market share (%)	Annual market penetration (%)	Purchase frequency (average)
Suave Naturals	12	19	2.0
Pantene Pro-V	10	16	1.9
Alberto VO5	6	11	1.6
Garnier Fructis	5	9	1.7
Dove	4	8	1.5
Finesse	1	2	1.4
Average			**1.7**

Note: Smaller US shampoo brands suffer from only slightly lower loyalty.

Source: Nielsen.

Snapshots of market share shifts over time (in the US, Canada and UK) also show double jeopardy: brands grow primarily by increasing their market penetration (Anschuetz, 2002; Baldinger, Blair & Echambadi, 2002; Stern & Ehrenberg, 2003). Shorter-term dynamic analysis by Andrew Ehrenberg and Colin McDonald (2003) showed that in 157 cases of small annual market share change the double jeopardy law was clear: both rising and declining brands displayed more change in their penetration than in their purchase frequency. Among the submissions for the Advertising Effectiveness Awards—run by the Institute of Practitioners in Advertising (IPA)—82% reported large penetration growth, 6% reported both penetration and loyalty growth, and only 2% reported loyalty growth alone. While a meta-analysis of 207 US split-cable advertising weight tests concluded that only one of the measured strategy variables was correlated with larger sales effects—this winning strategy was having an objective of increasing penetration (Lodish et al., 1995, p. 130).

A quantitative guide for growth targets

The double jeopardy law tells us what our marketing metrics will look like—*if we are successful* in gaining sales and market share. If Finesse (see Table 2.4) were to catapult up to the sales level of Suave Naturals or Pantene, it would be substantially more popular with millions more households buying it each year. But these households would not, on average, buy it much more often than current Finesse households buy the brand.

Finesse's brand manager could plan to reach market leadership by getting current customers to buy eight times a year. That would be enough to do it—in theory. But in practice that is impossible. Finesse-buying households currently only buy shampoo six times a year; therefore Finesse would need to command 100% loyalty just to achieve six purchases per year per customer. But no shampoo brand in the US is bought six times a year and no shampoo brand commands 100% loyalty. Such a marketing plan is fantasy. Double jeopardy tells us what is, and what isn't achievable.

Some managers find it difficult to accept that there is a scientific law constraining what they can achieve. But the law leaves plenty of room for marketing creativity. In the same way that laws of physics constrain the creativity of architects in a good way (they wish to design buildings that stand up to gravity, wind and rain), the double jeopardy law simply provides a practical guide to strategy formulation.

PENETRATION—THE WINNING TARGET

A recent analysis (Binet & Field, 2007) of 880 entries to the IPA's Effectiveness Awards showed that winners were far more likely to have set targets to increase market penetration. Each entrant stated its primary business purpose: for 178 entrants, this was 'customer retention/increase loyalty', while for 79 entrants it was 'new customer acquisition/penetration'. Here's how the awards played out:

Table 2.5: Analysis of the IPA's Effectiveness Awards

	Target to increase	
	Penetration (%)	**Loyalty (%)**
Gold winners	21	2
Silver winners	20	6
Bronze winners	18	3
No medal	41	89

Source: Binet & Field, 2007.

Campaigns that, unfashionably, aimed to increase penetration were twice as likely to report very large improvements in all hard measures of effectiveness including sales and profits. But only half the number of submissions aimed to increase penetration as aimed for loyalty/retention improvements. Therefore, marketers are using the wrong behavioural targets.

Les Binet, chairman of the judges, who completed this analysis, confessed to me that he once wrote a submission where he and his client aimed to increase penetration in the north and loyalty in the south. Annoyingly, while loyalty did improve in the south, penetration there improved even more. Try as one might, if you are successful in gaining sales it's unlikely you'll break the double jeopardy law.

And the Effectiveness Awards results remind us that it is a better strategy to go with the law than against it. Jim Nyce, previously Insights Director at Kraft, describes this as 'swimming downstream'. An analysis by his Consumer Insight & Strategy department (led by Frank Cotignola) showed that 56% of their brand plans were trying to 'swim upstream' by raising purchase frequency, while an internal study of the growth and decline patterns of 67 Kraft brands showed that penetration was the dominant driver of sales and share, in line with the double jeopardy law.

What about niche brands?

The term 'niche' is used loosely in marketing; often it is used to just mean small.[5] This turns out to be appropriate because most niche brands *are* small. Technically, a niche brand in a category should, for its market share, have an unusually small base of buyers who are unusually loyal.[6] If every category had a number of these brands, and/or their differences truly were substantial then the double jeopardy pattern wouldn't exist. There are far fewer niche brands than people expect, and they are less niche than we think.

What about cross-selling?

Another route to sales growth is to encourage current customers to buy different products. Customer relationship management (CRM) systems and loyalty programs often promise this benefit. It's widely viewed that this is an easy path to growth: you already have a relationship with these buyers, if they are made a good offer they should take it up. Yet many large corporations make good offers to their own employees and are disappointed by the response rate. If selling new products to your own employees is difficult, then cross-selling to existing customers might not be so easy after all.

Cross-selling metrics are another measurement of loyalty, so once again we find the double jeopardy law applies. There is little difference in cross-selling metrics between competing brands, and the small differences that do exist tend to reflect market share—not whether or not they have dedicated cross-selling programs.

---

5   A cynic would say the term was invented to replace the word 'small' because most brand managers are in charge of small brands. If you tell someone you meet at a party, 'I'm brand manager for X', and they say, 'Oh, I've never heard of X', what would you rather reply: 'That's because it's a small brand, it isn't bought by many people, and even these people don't buy it very often', or 'That's because it's a niche brand, with a very particular (discerning) client base'?

6   Theoretically a niche brand can be any size: small market share would be more probable, but a large market share niche brand would be theoretically possible. In reality niche brands are rare, but do come in all sizes, just mostly very small.

Tables 2.6 and 2.7 provide data on cross-selling metrics for insurance and banking, respectively.

Table 2.6: Cross-selling metrics for insurance

Insurance providers (Australia)	Market penetration (%)	Average number of products held by each customer
RAA	16	1.5
CGU	14	1.4
SGIC	13	1.5
AAMI	9	1.5
APIA	6	1.4
Average	12	1.5

Source: Mundt, Dawes & Sharp, 2006, pp. 465–569.

Table 2.7: Cross-selling metrics for banking

Personal banking (Australia)	Market penetration (%)	Average number of products held by each customer
Commonwealth Bank	29	2.0
ANZ Bank	18	2.1
Westpac Bank	14	2.2
National Australia Bank	13	2.3
Average	19	2.1

Source: Mundt, Dawes & Sharp, 2006, pp. 465–569.

The insurance data shows very little difference in the success of cross-selling by the competing brands. In banking there is a little more variation, but oddly there appears to be a slight reverse of the double jeopardy pattern where the two smaller brands have marginally higher customer loyalty. This is due to the two smaller brands being skewed towards business banking and having a consumer base of wealthier customers who hold more financial products overall, while the two larger brands are particularly successful in one product (e.g. credit cards), and this success gives them slightly more customers than expected—customers who hold just one product with them. So their deficient cross-selling metric is actually due to their unusual success (in one part of the market). In other words, we see no evidence of excellence in cross-selling.

In both markets there is very little difference between brands. Every insurance brand has a customer base that, on average, buys one and a half services from them; each banking brand's customers buy two services.

None of this says that cross-selling is impossible, but it implies that it is nowhere near as easy as textbooks make out, nor is it necessarily a route to huge sales gains. The lack of difference among the brands shown in Tables 2.6 and 2.7 suggests that dramatically changing cross-selling metrics is difficult and expensive (some brands have tried, but you wouldn't know it from looking at their results).

One reason it is harder than expected to cross-sell products to existing buyers is that those who haven't bought these products from you don't need them; for example, you can't sell car insurance to someone who drives a company car. Another reason is that service brands often already enjoy high loyalty; for example, most of your customers who needed a home loan came to you already (and you either gave them one or turned them down). Improving this already high loyalty rate is difficult.

Grow your base—but how?

So the double jeopardy law tells us, over and over again, that market share increases depend on substantially growing the size of your customer base. But how do customer bases grow? In the next chapter we look at more laws of growth.

FURTHER READING

Those interested in delving deeper, or simply seeing the wide range of conditions under which the double jeopardy law has been documented should read:

Ehrenberg, A, Goodhardt, G & Barwise, P 1990, 'Double jeopardy revisited', *Journal of Marketing*, vol. 54 (July), pp. 82–91.

Ehrenberg, A 1991, 'Politicians' double jeopardy: a pattern and exceptions', *Journal of the Market Research Society*, vol. 33, no. 1, pp. 347–53.

Bhat, S & Fox, R 1996, 'An investigation of jeopardy effects in store choice', *Journal of Retailing and Consumer Services*, vol. 3, no. 3, pp. 129–33.

Solgaard, H, Smith, D & Schmidt, M 1998, 'Double jeopardy patterns for political parties', *International Journal of Public Opinion Research*, vol. 10, no. 2.

Michael, JH & Smith, PM 1999, 'The theory of double jeopardy: an example from a forest products industry', *Forest Products Journal*, vol. 49, no. 3, pp. 21–6.

McDowell, WS & Dick, SJ 2005, 'Revealing a double jeopardy effect in radio station audience behavior', *Journal of Media Economics*, vol. 18, no. 4, pp. 271–84.

Sharp, B & Riebe, E 2005, 'Does triple jeopardy exist for retail chains?', *Journal of Empirical Generalisations in Marketing Science*, vol. 9.

Wright, M, Sharp, A & Sharp, B 1998, 'Are Australasian brands different?', *Journal of Brand and Product Management*, vol. 7, no. 6, pp. 465–80.

How to Grow Your Customer Base

Byron Sharp

What happens when brands grow or decline?

Double jeopardy tells us that when brands improve their market share their buyer base enlarges. This increase in customer franchise could be due to improvements in customer acquisition, but it could also be the result of reduced customer defection. It's a fact of marketing life that each year you lose buyers. If a brand can improve its retention levels then it should grow its customer base.

So in theory it's possible to grow your customer base by improving either retention or acquisition, or a combination of both. We'd expect that making customers more satisfied might bring about both, especially retention. There is now a large body of literature based on this assumption.

This raises the strategic question of whether marketers should emphasise retention or acquisition. Modern marketing ideology says retention is cheaper than acquisition. But is it? And what returns are possible? How much emphasis should be placed on retention versus acquisition?

Is retention cheaper?

A widely read *Harvard Business Review* article by Reichheld and Sasser (1990) states that customer defections can have a 'surprisingly powerful impact on the bottom line … companies can boost profits by almost 100% by retaining just 5% more of their customers'. This is a surprising, fantastic claim, and it turns out to be just that—pure fantasy.

It's reasonably presumed that this claim is based on empirical research, but Reichheld and Sasser's (1990) statement is merely based on a thought experiment; and it goes like this:

> Suppose a credit card company loses 10% of its customers each year, then the average customer life would be 10 years. Now if that firm were able to reduce its annual customer defection to 5% then the average customer tenure would double to 20 years. Given that a customer delivers some profits each year, now they stay for more years they must each give more.

Therefore, this is an analytical tautological 'finding', not a real-world discovery based on observing the results of retention efforts. It's similar to saying that if you win the lottery then you'll be richer: true by definition but hardly surprising.

Reichheld and Sasser (1990) presented their logic in a misleading manner because:

a Their 5% drop in defection is actually a drop of 5 *percentage points*, i.e. from 10% to 5%, which is a 50% decrease; a halving of customer defection.

b Their thought experiment wasn't about company profitability, it was about 'customer profitability', which is different. Essentially all they revealed is that if a customer stays (i.e. buys) for longer, then they give you more money over this longer period.[1]

---

1   This is not hidden in the *Harvard Business Review* article; while it is fair to accuse of Reichheld and Sasser of misleading language, they do clearly show how they reached their conclusion.

Given that Reichheld and Sasser's (1990) article was about profitability we might expect that they would have included some assumptions about costs, and they did. They simply assumed that the halving of defection is achieved at zero cost!

And finally they assume that halving customer defection in the real world is perfectly possible. Indeed, why stop at half? Their article was titled 'Zero defections …' Can companies radically alter their rate of customer defection? Is it possible to reduce defections to zero, or even to halve defections? Empirical evidence shows that this is wishful fantasy.

Customer defection rates follow double jeopardy

No doubt you have heard the old maxim that it costs five times as much to win a new customer as it does to stop one leaving. There is no empirical support for this idea. In reality, permanently reducing defection rates is difficult and expensive—because defection rates (another loyalty measure) also follow the double jeopardy law.

This means that a brand's defection rate is essentially a function of its market share, and the category it's in. This defection level doesn't vary significantly between competing brands.

How many customers a brand loses in a year depends on how many it has to lose in the first place. Obviously a brand can't lose a million customers if it doesn't have a million customers to start with. Larger brands therefore can, and do, lose more customers each year, and they also gain more customers. But as a proportion of their customer base they lose (and gain) less than smaller brands, i.e. their defection percentage is lower.

Imagine a two-brand market. One brand is smaller with 20% market share (a customer base of 200 customers); the other larger brand has 80% market share (a customer base of 800 customers). If the two brands maintain their respective share of customers, then each brand's defections must equal its acquisitions. Imagine the large brand loses (and gains) 100 customers each year. Then, in this two-brand market, the small brand must also lose and gain 100 customers (see Figure 3.1). The small brand's defection level is 50% (100 divided by 200) while the larger brand's defection level is only 12.5% (100 divided by 800).

Figure 3.1: More of the small brand's customer base turns over

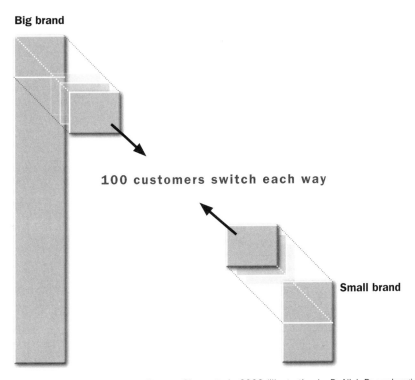

Source: Sharp et al., 2002 (illustration by Dr Nick Danenberg).

In real markets there are more than two brands, so things are more complicated. But the fundamental pattern, the double jeopardy law, still holds with brands with a larger market share having slightly lower defection levels (i.e. higher loyalty).

The double jeopardy law is a serious blow to Reichheld and Sasser's (1990) idea of easily and cheaply halving customer defection. Double jeopardy shows that it isn't possible to radically alter defection rates without massively shifting market share.

Look at Table 3.1, which shows defection rates for car brands in the US. The data comes from a survey of 10 000 new car buyers in the US in 1989–91. The survey recorded what car brand they bought and what brand they owned previously (if any). Defection levels are much higher than in most service industries, though still surprisingly low considering the dozens of other new car brands that each buyer could have bought rather than staying loyal. Each major car brand in the US suffers a defection rate of about 60–70%, or two-thirds of their customers. No brand has managed to obtain a defection rate vastly different from this average, and certainly not without having larger market share.

Table 3.1: Defection rates for car brands in the US, 1989–91

US automobile brand	Market penetration (%)	Defection rate (%)
Pontiac	9	58
Dodge	8	58
Chevolet	8	71
Buick	7	59
Ford	6	71
Toyota	6	70
Oldsmobile	5	66
Mercury	5	72
Honda	4	71
Average defection rate		**67**

Source: Bennett, 2005.

Table 3.2 is a similar table, showing defection rates for car brands in the UK. The data comes from a survey of 25 000 new car buyers in the UK and France in 1986–89. The survey recorded what car brand they bought and what brand they owned previously (if any). The UK and French markets are less fragmented than that in the US and the market shares of the reported brands are higher, and so, in line with the double jeopardy law, defection levels are lower.

Each brand suffers a defection rate of about 50% (i.e. a retention rate of also 50%). The double jeopardy pattern is again noticeable—the smaller brands have somewhat lower loyalty (higher defection rates). Ford, being the largest brand, has the lowest defection rate. But its defection level still isn't that much lower than its rivals.

Table 3.2: Defection rates for car brands in the UK and France, 1986–89

UK automobile brands	Penetration (%)	Defection (%)
Ford	27	31
Rover	16	46
GM	14	42
Nissan	6	45
VW/Audi	5	46
Peugeot	5	57
Renault	4	52
Fiat	3	50
Citroen	2	48
Toyota	2	50
Honda	1	53
Average defection rate		**47**

Source: Data kindly provided by Renault France, and fully described in Colombo, Ehrenberg & Sabavala, 2000.

Remember that Reichheld and Sasser assumed a cost-free halving of the defection level. It's difficult to see how it could be dirt cheap to do something that no other brand in the market has been able to do. Note that none of these brands has a defection rate around 25%, not even Ford, which has double the market share of its nearest competitor. Asking a brand like Honda to halve its defection rate is equivalent to asking it to increase its customer base more than thirtyfold! Doing things that no other brand has been able to do, in spite of considerable investments in customer relationship management (CRM) and other customer satisfaction initiatives, is seldom cheap or easy.

Amazing maths

The implications of the double jeopardy law for growth potential are profound, and can be shown with simple maths. Consider Tables 3.1 and 3.2 above. Each year a car brand gains about half its sales from new customers and about half from returning customers. If a brand like Toyota were to reduce its defection rate to zero then it would gain 50% more sales, which is one percentage point of market share. This one point is the maximum it can gain from improving retention. But each year about half of new car buyers switch brands, so each year 50 points of market share are up for grabs. This is the most Toyota can gain from improving acquisition, i.e. 50 times the sales potential that retention offers!

Most service industries have defection levels far lower than these examples. Figures of 3–5% are quite normal, so even if a company could reduce defection to zero it would give them a sales gain of only a few percentage points. In market after market the potential gains from acquisition dwarf the potential gains from reducing defection.

Even growing brands lose customers

Halving defections is neither easy nor cheap, and permanently reducing customer defection to zero is fantasy. Also, the growth potential from customer acquisition is much higher.

The double jeopardy law describes normal markets where brands typically aren't growing or declining substantially. What about dynamics? What role does defection play in delivering growth? Does defection reduce dramatically while a brand is growing? Does acquisition rise dramatically? Or, does growth come from a combination of both? Is growth dependent on marketing strategy? It turns out that the answer to these questions is very simple: growth is due to extraordinary acquisition. Contraction is due to dismal acquisition.

Erica Riebe (2003) examined the dynamics of customer base growth and contraction in her doctoral research. She examined both growing and

declining pharmaceutical brands over 10 years.[2] For each brand she calculated the amount of acquisition and defection it should have had given the
market norm and the size of the brand (i.e. if a brand's customer base was
stable then its acquisition and defection levels should be equal, and will
depend on the size of the brand). She expected that growing brands might
show excess acquisition and lower-than-expected defection, i.e. together
these two factors would contribute to the growth in the customer base.
Surprisingly, she found that growth was almost entirely due to particularly
high acquisition. The declining brands showed a similar pattern but in
reverse: their defection rates were healthy and matched stable brands of
similar market share, but their acquisition rates were poor.

Riebe (2003) replicated this research in France (looking at shampoo
and chocolate bars). Using twelve months of panel data she compared
each panel member's favourite brand in the first six months with his or
her favourite in the second six months. This allowed Riebe to calculate, for
each brand, how many 'first brand loyals' it gained and lost. The shampoo
category turned out to be too stable, with the customer bases of the
brands not changing. But in the chocolate category, where there was some
movement, the same pattern was seen as in pharmaceuticals—customer
base growth was mostly due to excelling in acquisition.

This research was later extended with further analysis and Nielsen provided four-and-a-half years of banking data. Again, it was good customer
acquisition that led to growth, and poor acquisition that caused decline.

Is defection largely outside of marketer control?

A simple explanation for the pattern described above is that customer
defection is largely outside of marketer control—at least in terms of
being able to alter it with customer service and other such initiatives.

---

2   The pharmaceutical panel data was kindly provided by ISIS Research (now part
     of Synovate), covering ten years of anti-depressant prescribing by UK doctors. It
     is an extraordinary data set because it covers such a long time period and so many
     'purchases'—perfect for studying sales growth and decline.

There is some very good evidence to support this. Consider the following data (Table 3.3) on annual defection rates from financial institutions in Australia. This data shows a very typical double jeopardy pattern: *loyalty declines with market share*. In comparison to the huge variation in market shares (a thirtyfold difference between Adelaide Bank and CBA), defection rates vary little.

Table 3.3: Defection rates (Australian financial institutions)

Financial institution	Market share (%)	Defection (%)
CBA	32.0	3.4
Westpac	13.0	4.3
NAB	11.0	5.3
ANZ	10.0	4.3
STG	6.0	4.3
Bank SA	1.4	5.0
Adelaide Bank	0.8	7.0
Average defection rate		**4.8**

Source: Roy Morgan Research.

The smallest brand, Adelaide Bank, is a small regional bank with branches essentially only in Adelaide. CBA, the largest bank by a considerable margin, is thoroughly national with branches in every main city and regional centre. If someone moves from Adelaide to Sydney (about 20% of Australians move house each year) and if they banked with Adelaide Bank they now find themselves a very long way from the nearest Adelaide Bank branch. Hence, they are likely to switch to another bank, one with branches convenient to their new Sydney home. But if they had previously banked with CBA in Adelaide, odds are that they will have Sydney branches that are just as convenient as ever.

These differences in physical distribution seem to almost entirely explain the double jeopardy pattern in bank defection rates. So Adelaide

Bank's comparatively high defection level (double CBA's) is probably nothing to do with differences in customer satisfaction, nor any indicator of CBA having a superior retention program. It's simply that Adelaide Bank is smaller than CBA and has fewer branches, so it must have more defection. Therefore, Adelaide Bank[3] should not worry about its higher defection rate; there is practically nothing that can be done about it unless Adelaide Bank dramatically increases its market share.

It's not surprising that research examining the reasons for customer defection (Bogomolova & Romaniuk, 2005; Lees, Garland & Wright, 2007) has shown that much defection occurs for reasons entirely beyond the firm's control (e.g. moving house, no longer needing the service, being directed by head office, etc.). Then there is the fact that any brand faces a great deal of competition and competitors are constantly trying to lure customers away. No matter how much you look after your customers, every now and then a competitor has to get lucky.

Acquisition is not optional

It seems hardly revolutionary that customer acquisition should be essential for growth, yet this seems to often get forgotten with today's emphasis on targeting, database marketing, CRM and loyalty programs.[4] The real-world evidence is very clear: it is essential to acquire customers even to just maintain your brand. But what sort of customers should you seek to

---

3   Adelaide Bank is, and has been for a long while, a profitable well-performing bank. Contrary to Reichheld and Sasser's implication, its defection rate has not decimated its profits.

4   Reichheld is a consultant selling a loyalty consulting service; he does not disguise this. But academics have no excuse of citing his work without critical examination (the obvious faults in his work are there for anyone to read). Unfortunately, mainstream textbooks have slavishly hopped onto the loyalty bandwagon, for example, 'Many companies are realising the importance of customer retention and that the key to retaining and building market share is building relationships with loyal customers' (Belch & Belch, 2008).

acquire? All buyers aren't equal, so who to target—among both existing and potential buyers?

The next chapter reveals a law concerning heavy and light repeat buying. These regularities in consumer behaviour underpin the stark patterns concerning brands' marketing metrics we've seen in previous chapters.

Which Customers Matter Most?

Byron Sharp

The difficulty lies, not in the new ideas,
but in escaping the old ones.

John Maynard Keynes (quoted in Drexler, 1987)

Smart marketers know they need to reach all buyers (i.e. buyers of the category, and everyone from light to heavy buyers of a brand) in order to reinforce buying propensities, and to win new sales.

The death of mass marketing

> **MARKETING STRATEGIES**
>
> - **Mass marketing** is trying to sell to all buyers of the category; having many occasional buyers and accepting weak loyalty and relationships.
> - **Target marketing** is not trying to sell to all buyers of the category, but rather focusing on either heavier buyers of the brand, or a distinctive segment of people.

Phil Kotler and colleagues (1998), amongst others, has declared mass marketing to be oldfashioned. 'Modern' marketing is said to be about positioning; targeting segments; focusing on loyal, heavier buyers; focusing on retention (not acquisition) and return on investment (ROI). Oddly, textbooks have been preaching this 'new' message for decades. Today's fashionable media strategy uses new, diverse, low-reach media to deliver new 'consumer engagement'. Broad-reaching television channels and newspapers—while still very much used by marketers (to great effect)—are no longer de rigueur. Today the fashion is for loyalty programs, websites for loyalists (e.g. Budweiser's 'Bud.tv'), targeting 'influencers', customer relationship management (CRM) and 'new media'.

Yet buyers are busier than ever, and many brands are vying for their attention and custom. Forming deep relationships with a substantial number of buyers seems more unlikely than ever. Consequently, it is logical to expect marketers to strive to become better at mass marketing, rather than abandoning it. This is supported by researchers who have been studying patterns in buyer behaviour and brand performance; they have concluded that mass marketing is essential for both brand maintenance and growth.

For decades marketing scientists have been studying buying rates and the statistical distribution of these rates. Buying rates show how many people buy a brand once a year, how many buy it twice, three times and so on. The patterns in these buying rates are rarely taught at business schools but they are used everyday in businesses. For example, these law-like patterns underpin successful sales-forecasting techniques that are used by leaders in this field like BASES, and they are also integrated into some media scheduling models.

Today we know a lot about how often people buy, and how much variation there is between people's buying. We know that buyers differ from one another in terms of how often they buy and the different brands they buy. We also know how many of each type (weight) of buyer there are. These data provide benchmarks, allow for very useful predictions and deliver great insights. This is a tremendous scientific achievement, and something all marketers should be familiar with.

Light buyers matter

All brands have many lighter buyers. While these people are only occasional buyers of a brand, there are so many of them that they significantly contribute to sales volume.

It is surprising just how light the typical buyer is. Let's look at a super big brand in a frequently bought category: Coca-Cola (see Figure 4.1). In many markets, Coke is the market leader by far in the cola category. Data from the TNS Impulse panel in the UK (TNS tracks personal purchases, for example, a person buying a can of Coke to drink themself) shows that the average Coca-Cola buyer purchases almost 12 times a year, around once a month. But this average is very misleading, because purchase frequencies show a skewed distribution. The average buyer is not typical. There are some people who buy Coca-Cola morning, noon and night—that's more than 1000 purchases every year. So for Coca-Cola to have an average buying rate of just 12, each of these super heavy buyers must be balanced by many hundreds of Coke buyers who buy only a few times a year.

The TNS data shows that a typical Coca-Cola buyer purchases (for him- or herself) just one or two cans or bottles a year. That's half of all Coke buyers. Only a tiny fraction of Coke buyers purchase around the average amount of 12 purchases. Therefore, the average buyer is certainly not typical.

Around 30% of cola buyers don't even buy themselves a single Coca-Cola each year. Note that these are people who do buy cola (not just soft drink)—so most of these people do indeed buy Coca-Cola, just very occasionally and not every year!

Therefore, from Coca-Cola's perspective, a heavy buyer is anyone who buys herself three or more cans or bottles of Coke a year. Many of us who thought we hardly every bought Coke now turn out to be quite normal Coke buyers. Very light buyers dominate, even for Coca-Cola—which is a very large brand indeed.

Figure 4.1: Percentage of UK cola buyers purchasing Coke x times, 2005

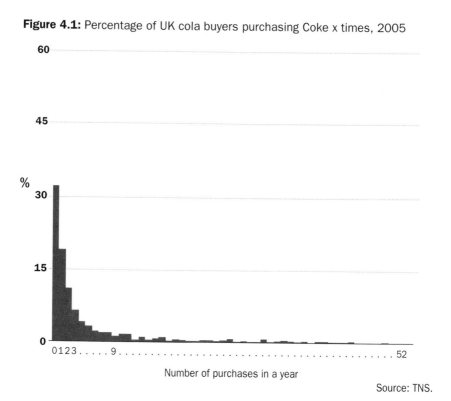

Number of purchases in a year

Source: TNS.

What do the buying frequencies look like for smaller brands? They are surprisingly similar. Let's look at Pepsi, which is a considerably smaller brand in this market (see Figure 4.2).

The average Pepsi buyer in this market buys only nine times a year, which is somewhat lighter than the average Coca-Cola buyer (c.f. 12). There are many more cola buyers who don't buy Pepsi in a year—more than 50%, compared to the 30% who didn't buy Coke that year. This is because Pepsi is a smaller brand. But again, a heavy buyer for Pepsi is anyone who buys more than three times a year.

Is the UK cola market strange? What does the US look like? Figure 4.3 shows the purchasing pattern (this time at household level) of Coke in the US in 2007. The UK and US buying patterns are astonishingly similar because this pattern generalises around the world, over time, across product categories, and for all the different market research providers.

Figure 4.2: Percentage of UK cola buyers purchasing Pepsi x times, 2005

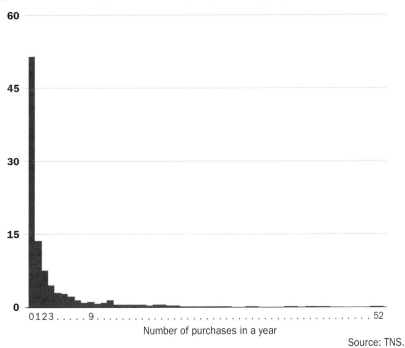

Number of purchases in a year

Source: TNS.

Figure 4.3: Percentage of US households purchasing Coke x times, 2007

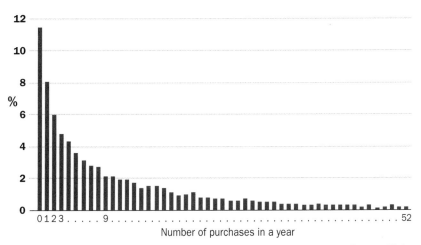

Number of purchases in a year

Source: Nielsen.

So brands have many light buyers who buy the brand very occasionally. They buy the brand infrequently because they don't buy from the category very often, and they buy a number of different brands. For example, it's very common for a high-volume, packaged goods category to be bought on average less than 10 times a year by buyers.[1] Brands in such categories are only bought by their consumers three or four times a year on average. For such a brand their most typical buyers buy them barely more than once a year.

Marketers easily forget how rarely their buyers buy their brand. They are often surprised how low their *average purchase frequency* metric is (and they mistakenly conclude that this means there is plenty of scope to easily increase this metric). Few appreciate that this average is still much heavier than their typical buyer—and that the calculation of the average doesn't include all those who happened to not purchase the brand at all during the period. The great mass of typical buyers only very occasionally buy a brand.

This shows up in services markets too, where a large proportion of customers buy most of their purchases from another brand. For example, in personal banking, almost half a bank's customers will list another bank as their main financial institution.

At the other end of the buying spectrum there are a few buyers who buy a category often—and a few of these buy a category very often. These buyers are important because they deliver a lot of sales volume in spite of their small numbers. For example, the 4% or so of Coca-Cola's buyers who purchase Coke once a week or more (52+ times a year) deliver almost a quarter of its yearly sales volume.

Fortunately, these heavy buyers are comparatively easy to market to, because the category and the brand are, comparatively speaking, much more important to them than to the typical buyer. These heavy buyers get many opportunities to see point-of-sale material and packaging changes

---

1   Category purchase rates also show a skewed distribution. While the average buyer might purchase from the category 10 times, the typical category buyer purchases from the category just a few times a year.

(and they are presumably very good at learning about regular promotions). These buyers are also far more receptive to the brand's advertising: they notice it more and they find it easier to process and remember.

At the very extreme, the buyer who drinks Coca-Cola morning, noon and night has a very well ingrained habit. They are locked in their ways and may even be a little bit addicted to the product.[2] One could argue there is little need to market to these buyers at all, especially considering that they are comparatively non-responsive to advertising (i.e. their behaviour tends not to change in response to advertising; their buying neither increases nor decreases). They will keep buying in large volumes until one day something momentous happens and they downgrade, or drop the brand, or quit the category (or die), all of which is usually out of your control.

At the other end of the buying spectrum are the typical, very infrequent buyers. These people—who are most of your consumers—are a marketing challenge because it is hard to justify spending money on them individually (direct mail is usually out of the question). And yet collectively they are important for sales volume and offer great potential for growth. An implication of the skewed distribution of buying rates is that to maintain sales a brand needs to reach out to these masses of buyers. For two reasons:

1 there are so many of them
2 they buy so infrequently and could easily forget about you.

Pareto's law (but not as you know it)

You may be wondering if this distribution of buying frequencies has something to do with marketing's best-known law: 80% of sales come from the top 20% of brand buyers. Yes it does, it underpins Pareto's '80/20' law. However, it is important to know that the '80/20 law' is a misleading simplification. The ratio is rarely as extreme as 80/20.

---

2   Soft drinks that contain caffeine may show slightly higher repeat-purchase rates (i.e. higher loyalty).

The share of purchases undertaken by the heaviest 20% of a brand's buyers (the 'Pareto share') reflects the polarisation in buying rates between the heaviest and lightest buyers. In our Coca-Cola example, there are plenty of cola buyers who buy themselves a Coca-Cola only a few times a year, and a smaller group who buy much more regularly (once a week or daily or more). This results in a typical Pareto share.

In contrast, there are categories where buyers are more homogeneous. For example, most people fill their car with petrol once a week. There is a tiny group of people who don't own a car, yet who occasionally buy fuel when they hire a car—but only a few of these people show up in a period of analysis. There are some other people who drive a lot, and fill up twice, maybe three times a week. But the vast majority of people buy petrol once a week (and even the heavy buyers don't buy significantly more than this), so buying rates aren't polarised and the Pareto share is not very extreme.

The Pareto share metric depends on the time period of study (Schmittlein, Cooper & Morrison, 1993). In a very short time period all the people who have bought the brand will have bought at a very similar rate; for example, in a week almost everyone who has bought has done so just once, perhaps a few have bought twice, in which case the heaviest 20% of buyers will be responsible for about 20% of sales (say 25/20). As time goes by the heaviest buyers reveal their true colours and show how much more frequently they buy the brand. Also, larger numbers of very light buyers enter the analysis window by buying the brand just once. This increases the polarisation between heavy and light buyers—giving a more extreme Pareto share metric.

Our research (Sharp, B & Romaniuk, 2007) of many dozens of brands, across product categories, shows that over a three-month period a 'fast-moving consumer good' brand will typically have a Pareto share of only 35%. Over a year this metric will have risen to over 50%, usually not far over 50%[3] and rarely anything like the proverbial 80%.

---

3   Such 'heavy half' patterns led to Professor Gerald Goodhardt's 20:30:50 law, which states that the 20% heaviest buyers account for 50% of purchases, the 50% lightest buyers account for 20% of purchases, and so the middle 30% of buyers account for 30% of purchases, i.e. 20:30:50 buyers accounting for 50:30:20 purchases.

Table 4.1 shows that brands within a category have a similar Pareto share. This doesn't vary a great deal between categories. Table 4.2 contains 2007 Nielsen BrandScan data reporting the average Pareto shares for brands in a selection of US product categories. To show how this pattern generalises across countries, Table 4.3 shows some similar product categories in South Africa and Australia.

Table 4.1: Pareto share for brands in the body spray and deodorant category

Brand	Market share (%)	Percentage volume accounted for by heaviest 20% of buyers	
		3 months	12 months
Sure	16	42	53
Lynx	14	41	53
All others	14	40	51
Impulse	8	45	55
Soft & Gentle	7	39	52
Rightguard	7	39	51
Dove	6	36	48
Tesco	4	43	53
Vaseline	3	39	51
Asda	3	42	54
Adidas	3	35	45
Gillette Series	3	39	50
Other brands	3	39	49
Physio Sport	2	37	50
Sanex	2	35	45
Nivea	2	36	46
Wilkinsons	1	41	54
Arrid	1	37	45
Natrel Plus	1	35	47
Mum	1	35	46
Average		39	50

Brands within a category have a similar pareto share (Sharp & Romaniuk 2007)
Data Source: Kantar Worldpanel.

Table 4.2: Pareto shares for brands in a selection of US product categories

Product	Brand average (%)
Dog food—moist	56
Dog food—wet	65
Cat food—wet	64
Yoghurt—refrigerated	60
Creme rinses and conditioners	47
Cat food—dry	56
Fabric softeners—liquid	51
Dog food—dry	54
Deodorants—aerosol	48
Deodorants—cologne	48
Yellow fats	53
Detergents—light duty	49
Cat food—moist	46
Shampoo etc.	42
Breakfast cereals	54
Automatic dishwasher compounds	45
Deodorants—stick/solid	46
Canned soup	53
Fabric softners—dry	43
Deodorants—roll on	44
Fabric softners—aerosol	35
Soft drinks	64
Average	**51**

Source: Sharp & Romaniuk 2007, Data Source: The Nielsen Company.

Table 4.3: Australia and South Africa Pareto share results

Australia	Category (%)	Brand average (%)
Yellow margarine	42	60
Cereals	46	60
Soup	52	53
Shampoo	55	46
Conditioner	51	48
Washing detergent—liquid	54	53
Washing detergent—powder	44	48
Automatic dishwashing	39	42
Yoghurt and dairy desserts	49	64
Carbonated soft drinks	53	65
Deodorants	48	51
Cat food—dry	44	57
Cat food—wet	43	66
Average	**48**	**55**

South Africa	Category (%)	Brand average (%)
Yellow margarine	42	53
Defined cereals	44	48
Hot cereal	48	49
Detergents	35	48
Dishwashing liquids	47	50
Automatic dishwashing products	65	59
Soft drinks	56	56
Canned soup	49	36
Regular foil packet soup	45	46
Shampoo and conditioner	60	47
Average	**49**	**49**

Source: Sharp & Romaniuk 2007, Data Source: The Nielsen Company.

If 80% of your buyers delivered only 20% of your annual sales, it would be tempting to ignore them. But if these light buyers deliver around half your sales, do you still want to ignore them? Marketing's Pareto law is important, but the ratio isn't 80/20 and the traditional implications are incorrect.

Normally the Pareto law is used to justify a strategy that concentrates on the brand's heaviest buyers (e.g. Koch, 1999). This strategy has some merit. These buyers are worth more, and marketers can justify spending more per buyer. But making them the dominant focus of marketing activity is not wise. Ignoring light and non-buyers of a brand is no recipe for growth (as we saw in the Chapters 2 and 3).

Buyers aren't always what they seem

The logic of targeting heavy buyers is undermined further by the fact that the *future* sales potential of individuals is different than their current buying suggests. This is true even when you have perfectly reliable sales data on your individual buyers, and even when there is no real change in their behaviour. Non-buyers and light buyers are heavier buyers than you think, and heavy buyers are lighter. This is neatly illustrated in a two-year analysis of a leading brand of tomato sauce in the US using IRI and AC Nielsen panel data (Anschuetz, 2002). Although the brand was stationary (not growing or losing sales volume), 14% of its sales came from households that did not buy it at all in the year before; in other words, from people who the brand's marketing team would have considered were non-buyers of the brand. While the small group (9%) of heavy buying households delivered 34% of volume, which was less than the 43% they delivered in year 1. See Table 4.4 below, which shows that over time the heavier buyers get lighter, and the non-buyers and light buyers get heavier.

The way the lightest buyers became heavier and the heaviest buyers became lighter is a 'regression to the mean' phenomenon. This law (which we'll call 'the law of buyer moderation')[4] applies to all brands and can be precisely predicted from the known distribution of buying frequencies.

---

4   See pages vii–viii for a list of the laws and discoveries introduced in this book.

Table 4.4: Sales volumes from different buyer groups one year later

Buyer group	Percentage of sample	Buying frequency in year 1	Representing brand sales volume (%)	
			Year 1	Year 2
Non-buyers	44	0	0	14
Light buyers	22	1	14	16
Moderate buyers	25	2–4	43	36
Heavy buyers	9	5+	43	34
Total	**100**		**100**	**100**

Source: Anschuetz, 2002; US IRI panel data.

In fact, few of these buyers are actually changing, which can seem rather mysterious, and is widely misunderstood. Most people don't know about the law of buyer moderation. This law undermines marketers' strategies to target heavy buyers of a brand and ignore light buyers (and the great deal of sales potential that they offer).

The law of buyer moderation occurs because of variation in the timing of individuals' purchasing. Some years buyers purchase the brand once, other years they buy it twice as much—this isn't real change; there is simply a (predictable) degree of wobble even around a stable ongoing buying rate. This wobble means that some of the households that were called 'non-buyers of the brand' weren't really—they just hadn't bought in the particular base year and so were misclassified as non-buyers. Just as some buyers were misclassified as light buyers when they really were heavier. Other customers were misclassified as heavy buyers because they bought the brand a bit more often than usual in the year the analyst chose to classify them (perhaps relatives came to visit so one year they had to buy extra). This phenomenon is much worse over short periods (a month or a quarter) than over a year, though it still occurs in annual data, and even for a big brand, as Table 4.4 above shows.

So we have three key facts about marketing's Pareto law:

1 It is law-like and applies across brands and categories.
2 It's not as severe as 80/20.
3 The analytical time period affects Pareto metrics and targeting based on customer value. Put simply, next period your heaviest 20% of customers won't be so heavy, the light buyers will be heavier, and some of the non-buyers will buy. This is the law of buyer moderation.

However, there is another law-like pattern that, in Professor Andrew Ehrenberg's (2004) words, 'should have been the end of the marketing pipe-dream of just recruiting heavy-buying buyers'. Let's look at what happens to a brand's distribution of buying rates when the brand grows its market share.

Changes occur across heavy and light segments

Look again at Figures 4.1 and 4.2, which show the buying frequencies of Coke and Pepsi buyers.

The shape of the distributions is very similar—going from Coke to Pepsi it looks as if the frequencies have simply slid to the left (i.e. everyone buying a little less frequently). In fact, both these distributions have the same mathematical properties; this type of distribution is called a negative binomial distribution (NBD). NBD seems to describe the purchase frequencies of all brands, and has done so for decades (it was discovered in 1959 by Andrew Ehrenberg). The NBD is typically a very skewed distribution with a 'long tail' (i.e. there are many more buyers who are lighter than the average buyer). Hence, there is a 60/20 Pareto concentration of sales volume.

This large proportion of very light buyers shows up in brand perform-ance metrics (as we saw in Chapters 2 and 3). Remember that brands with larger market share typically have substantially higher penetration figures than smaller brands (the double jeopardy law). But in contrast, the purchase frequency scores of the larger brands (how often their buyers buy their brand) are only marginally higher. And when brands grow or decline there is a lot of change in their category penetration (the size of their buyer base) and little change in their purchase frequency. Now we can see the reason why the penetration metric shows so much change. It's due to the NBD's skewed distribution of buying rates. When a brand grows it recruits a lot of light buyers who become heavy enough to buy at least once during the period of analysis; so now they show up in the penetration metric. More heavier buyers also buy more frequently, but overall the average rate of buying doesn't change much (see how little the mean average differs in the Coke and Pepsi charts). Therefore, the NBD explains the double jeopardy law.

One of the great insights is that all brands, irrespective of their size, face an NBD distribution of heavy to light buyers. When brands grow, or decline in market share, they simply move from one weight of this distribution to another. Put another way, changes in sales come from buying propensities changing across the entire market—from heavy to light and non-buyers of the brand. Every buyer group (or weight) changes.[5] When marketing is successful in delivering more sales and market share, it does so by giving the brand more heavy buyers, more medium buyers and a lot more light buyers. This means that for maintenance or growth, a brand's marketing has to somehow, at least over time, reach all the buyers in a category.

Sales growth won't come from relentlessly targeting a particular segment of a brand's buyers. Yet this targeting fantasy continues to appear in marketing plans and underpins the use of loyalty ladders and other market research products (e.g. the Conversion Model). This fantasy is harming marketing effectiveness.

When marketing successfully increases a brand's market share, buying propensities change across the board. This tells us that marketing has the

---

5   This doesn't mean that every single buyer changes his or her buying frequency, though usually many do. It means that every group of buyers shows some changes. Hence, the idea of targeting a particular group (and just affecting this particular group) runs counter to what actually occurs in the real world.

best chance of being successful when it has as much reach as possible. Marketing is particularly successful when it reaches light and non-buyers of a brand.

Therefore, marketing that seeks to increase sales by targeting heavier buyers is unlikely to succeed. Loyalty programs are a classic example of a strategy skewed towards heavier buyers of a brand. These programs are very popular with marketers; and yet with thousands of such programs running it is difficult to find any claiming great success. The serious academic studies report the same finding: loyalty programs generate small or no shifts in market share (see Chapter 11). Price promotions, in contrast, do increase sales, but they are also skewed towards heavier buyers. In spite of a lot of volume being sold on deal, promotions stimulate only small amounts of incremental volume (see Chapter 10). Many of the sales would have occurred anyway, and marketers can seldom afford to keep the promotion going for long periods. When the price promotion ends, sales instantly collapse back to their normal level. This is a good example of how difficult it is to bring about sustained growth by targeting only heavy buyers. If this weren't the case, then we would routinely see brands that had different buying distributions, and unusually high loyalty metrics for their market share levels. But we don't.

Conversely, marketing that targets light buyers of the brand, and/or non-buyers, has far greater chance of success. This is because such marketing has great reach: most of a brand's buyers are light buyers, and because it's nearly impossible to simply target light buyers, heavy buyers tend to get hit too (because heavy buyers are far more likely to notice advertising, visit stores and read publicity).

A classic example of brand growth is due to winning distribution in a new geographical area. This reaches buyers who, because it was inconvenient for them, were previously light buyers (or even real non-buyers) of the brand. These previously light/non-buyers start buying the brand and its penetration metric jumps up. The new store also improves the availability of the brand for existing heavier buyers, when they happen to be in the neighbourhood. This is now a great improvement in availability for them.

So they also buy a little more often. This helps nudge up average purchase frequency (and other loyalty metrics). This large rise in penetration and small gain in loyalty fits the double jeopardy pattern we saw in brand performance metrics in Chapter 2.

Conclusion

Now you know how brands grow and how marketing, when it is successful, affects buying rates. The implications counter much fashionable marketing thought, and yet are clear and simple:

1 Acquisition is vital for growth and maintenance.
2 Reaching all buyers is vital, especially light, occasional buyers of the brand.

This is a recipe for clever mass marketing, which is not surprising because it was mass marketing (not CRM, relationship marketing[6] or loyalty programs) that built the majority of today's leading brands. But it need not be a recipe for unsophisticated mass marketing. Reaching all potential buyers of a brand, at the right time and at low cost, is tricky and there is much to learn. The digital revolution is creating new opportunities to reach consumers in different ways, at different times—to be more relevant, and fit in better to their heterogeneous lives. There are great opportunities for sophisticated mass marketing.

Our next chapter is about learning about the buyers we have to reach. Who are they? How do we identify them?

---

6   One of the most successful new products of the twentieth century—and arguably the first genuinely effective drug—(Bayer's) aspirin was also the first to be marketed to physicians in the UK (they were each sent a letter). It is incorrect to portray this as a highly selective direct marketing program; this was a big advance in mass marketing. Much successful direct marketing today is mass marketing.

Our Buyers
Are Different

Byron Sharp

The good news is that your customers are just like your competitor's customers, and their customers are like yours. This means their buyers are up for grabs. So, target the whole market.

Who are our buyers? Who are our potential customers?

Common marketing ideology states that differentiated brands should sell to different groups of people, or should sell for different occasions or uses. In which case, an important question for brand managers is, 'What sort of people buy my brand?' The answer to this question provides insight into how to market a brand. It also allows for a brand's current sales potential to be estimated: if a brand sells to a unique customer base it can't sell to everyone and its growth potential has clear boundaries.

In 1959[1] a business school professor at the University of Hawaii gave personality tests to people who owned Ford and Chevrolet cars (see Evans, 1959). This sounds like an odd thing to do, but the theory was that Americans in the 1950s took their cars very seriously, cars were deeply

---

1   1959 was a good year for marketing science. The negative binomial distribution (NBD) of buying rates was discovered in the same year. See discussion of NBD discovery on pages 52 and 121.

symbolic purchases, and marketers had invested in building distinctive brand images. It was expected this would show up in interesting ways in the personality profiles of the respective customer bases. Executives from car companies and academics had expressed this belief.

The results were indeed interesting. The personality and demographic profiles of Ford and Chevrolet owners were essentially identical. The lack of difference shocked the marketing world. At first people argued about the results. Then the finding was repeatedly confirmed with different samples, techniques and product categories. After that everyone decided to ignore the discovery. As Winston Churchill said, 'Man will occasionally stumble over the truth, but usually manages to pick himself up, walk over or around it, and carry on.' (Klotz, 1996).

Nearly 50 years later a series of vastly more comprehensive studies were undertaken examining the profiles of the customer bases of competing brands. These studies profiled hundreds of brands, across dozens of categories (from cigarettes to computer games to mortgages) over time (Hammond, Ehrenberg & Goodhardt, 1996; Kennedy & Ehrenberg, 2000; Kennedy & Ehrenberg, 2001a; Kennedy & Ehrenberg, 2001b; Kennedy, McDonald & Sharp, 2000). Just as importantly, the studies used hundreds of variables capable of describing buyers: demographics, psychographics, attitudes, values and media habits. The key discovery of these studies is that competing brands sell to the same sort of people. Within each brand's customer base there is a lot of variation (i.e. different types of people), but each brand has the same variation.

Table 5.1 presents car ownership data from a different decade (1990s), but still the same pattern is clear. The customer bases of these UK car brands are quite similar to each other—even in the newspapers they read. Rover buyers, in spite of driving an up-market brand, still read the tabloid newspaper, the *Sun*, far more than they read the more intellectual newspaper, the *Telegraph*. This is also true for the owners of all the other car brands, and reflects the fact that the *Sun* is considerably more popular than the *Telegraph*. The greatest difference in the customer base is household size. This reflects the fact that larger households buy brands of cars that are physically bigger (more seats with a larger boot). Sierra and Cavalier are somewhat physically larger vehicles.

Table 5.1: Car brands sell to similar types of people, UK 1990s

Owners of	Gender (%)		Household size (%)		Owners who read newspapers (%)	
	Men	**Women**	**1–2 people**	**2+**	**Sun**	**Telegraph**
Rover	52	48	40	24	20	9
Escort	50	50	34	27	26	5
Sierra	50	50	25	34	28	4
Cavalier	51	49	29	33	24	6
Average	**51**	**49**	**31**	**30**	**25**	**6**

Source: TGI.

The similarities in the customer bases include the values that the different car owners hold. Table 5.2 shows a delightful collection of consumer values. Respondents may be fibbing when 98% of them say they don't judge people by the car they drive but, if so, your honesty doesn't depend on the brand of car you drive.

Table 5.2: Owners of different car brands hold similar values, UK 1990s

Owners of	I cannot bear untidiness	I keep up with technology	I judge people by the car they drive	A car is only to get from A to B
	% agreeing			
Rover	16	11	1	18
Escort	19	9	3	21
Sierra	17	9	2	17
Cavalier	17	10	3	17
Average	**18**	**10**	**2**	**18**

Source: TGI.

Let's look at beer brands in Canada (see Table 5.3).[2] In spite of the differences in price, origin (from Mexico to Toronto) and brand images, these beer brands have the same customer profiles. Modelo and Corona skew a little bit towards women and younger drinkers, but that's about the only difference that is substantive.

Table 5.3: Beer brands sales

Buyers of	Gender (%)		Age group (%)		Earnings ('000s)	
	Men	Women	<29	50–59	<$30	>$50
Coors	58	42	23	22	21	36
Canadian	71	29	30	19	26	35
Bud	67	33	32	19	30	27
Oland	69	31	34	17	24	38
Blue	69	31	30	20	28	28
Sleeman	71	29	24	20	18	40
Corona	52	48	34	13	24	35
Modelo	51	49	33	12	25	35
Miller	69	31	38	17	27	39
Average	64	36	31	18	25	35

Source: Data courtesy of Dee McGrath, Molson Breweries Canada; region and year hidden.

Now let's look at credit cards (see Table 5.4). These are in a product/ service category where there can be very substantial differences between products. These differences might appeal to particular market segments and not to others.

Again, the user profiles of the brands are very similar. Every credit card brand has a customer base that's about half female and half male. Barclays MasterCard has a customer base that is 60% male compared to

---

2   Data courtesy of Dee McGrath, Molson Breweries Canada; region and year hidden.

Table 5.4: Demographic profiles of credit card brands, UK

Credit card	Gender (%)		Age (years) (%)							
	Male	Female	15–19	20–24	25–34	35–44	45–54	55–64	65+
Barclaycard Visa	51	49	1	4	17	23	22	18	14
TSB Trust card	51	49	1	3	18	20	21	19	19
Access Natwest	54	47	1	2	16	24	23	21	14
Access Midlands	52	48	1	3	18	24	21	20	13
Barclays MasterCard	60	40	1	3	15	21	23	20	17
Access Lloyds	54	46	2	3	18	22	22	20	13
Bank of Scotland Visa	56	44	1	2	17	21	26	19	14
Midland Visa	53	48	1	2	15	24	24	19	15
TSB MasterCard	56	45	1	6	18	20	21	18	16
Co-op Bank Visa	56	44	2	2	17	17	23	20	20
Average brand	**54**	**46**	**1**	**3**	**17**	**22**	**22**	**19**	**16**

Source: TGI.

the average of 54%—but this is a small difference that has no practical marketing significance. No sensible marketer would alter their marketing strategy based on this data. Also, around 40% of every brand's customer base is aged between 35 and 54 years old; this percentage is 47% for Access Natwest—but again, this is a small difference that has no practical significance.

These sorts of minor difference—some simply due to random sampling variation—were the norm in all the research studies. This is illustrated in Table 5.5, which shows the average size of the average deviation from the brand norm in more than 40 product/service categories.

Table 5.5: Deviation from the brand norm

Category	Demo	Media	Values	Average
Cigarettes	4	4	6	6
Cat food	3	1	4	4
Mints	3	1	3	3
Toothbrushes	3	1	3	3
Private health insurance	4	2	3	3
Sweets	3	1	2	3
Crisps	3	1	3	3
Toilet soap	3	1	2	3
Package holidays	3	1	3	3
Dry batteries	3	1	2	3
Other chocolate	3	1	2	2
Kitchen rolls	3	1	3	2
Nuts	3	1	2	2
Chocolate bars	3	1	2	2
Toothpaste	2	1	2	2
Toilet paper	2	1	2	2

Table 5.5: Deviation from the brand norm (cont.)

Category	Demo	Media	Values	Average
Computers	3	2	2	2
Record shops	3	1	1	2
Store retail cards	3	1	2	2
Computer games	3	1	2	2
Vitamins	3	1	2	2
Liquid detergent	3	1	2	2
Grocers	3	1	2	2
Yogurt	3	1	2	2
Light bulbs	2	1	2	2
Car tyres	2	1	2	2
Stain removers	2	1	2	2
Car insurance	3	1	1	2
Coffee	2	1	2	2
Home contents	2	1	1	2
Paint	3	1	1	2
Shampoo	2	1	2	2
Airlines	2	1	1	1
Camera film	2	1	1	1
Headache tablets	2	1	1	1
Cars	2	1	1	1
Credit cards	2	1	1	1
Mortgages	2	1	1	1
Fuel	2	1	1	1
Retailers	1	1	1	1
Average	3	1	2	2

The categories are ranked by size of the deviation, but as you can see there isn't great variation between them. In each of these categories the typical deviation is small, apart from some rather obvious differences, such as:

- Scottish newspapers have more readers in Scotland than the average newspaper brand.
- Children's television channels have more children viewers than the average television channel (though still almost half the viewers of these channels are adults).
- Very expensive brands have fewer poor people in their customer base.

Large exceptions are worthy of management attention, but of course they are undoubtedly well known (e.g. that's why we use names like 'children's channels').

Extreme targeting

Maybe the real-world looks like this because marketers haven't targeted special audiences. Maybe if they tried harder reality might match textbook theory. But the two following case studies suggest that even when marketers try, in very overt ways, to target special audiences, they end up with normal-looking customer bases (so long as they are successful in winning market share). By definition, the more market share they gain, the more normal their customer base becomes.[3]

No girls

I first saw a Yorkie chocolate bar in a London corner store and was surprised by the packaging: it featured the slogan, 'It's not for girls!' and had a picture of a girl that was crossed out.[4] This packaging looks like a serious attempt to gain a segmented customer base: men.

---

3   The profile of a monopoly brand is identical to the category profile.
4   To see a visual of the Yorkie bar packaging, visit <http://en.wikipedia.org/wiki/Yorkie_(chocolate_bar)>.

Of course, this is cheeky British humour, designed to get the brand—and its television advertising—noticed.[5] However, decades before Nestlé adopted this slogan, Yorkie ads consistently stressed the large chunks of chocolate[6] and very much targeted blue-collar, male workers. [7] Most of the original advertising featured truck drivers enjoying Yorkie bars. After a long gap, or a period of unmemorable advertising, the 'It's not for girls!' campaign was launched—perhaps as a return to the brand's historic roots. As one commentator noted, 'From the ads they seem to be targeting not "British men" but British, large, bearded, macho, builders. That's got to be a limited market …' (Redfern, 2002). But either the market got the joke or the targeting failed because this is what the user base of Yorkie looks like today:

Table 5.6: Percentage of Yorkie bar buyers: male versus female over different product variants

Gender	Total brand	Yorkie—egg	Yorkie—honey-comb	Yorkie—milk	Yorkie—raisin & biscuit	Yorkie—roast almond	Yorkie—the nutter
Male	56	26	73	57	46	0	40
Female	44	74	27	43	54	100	60

Source: TNS.

Table 5.6 shows that the demographic breakdown fluctuates across Yorkie varieties, partly due to random sampling variation, but the obvious pattern is that a lot of women buy Yorkie—they make up about half of its customer base.

---

5   For an example of Yorke's television advertising, see <www.youtube.com/watch?v=ctpOxfA2gDY>.

6   Professor Gerald Goodhardt remembers that Yorkie was launched, by the company Rowntree (later bought by Nestle), at a time when chocolate had become very expensive and major players like Cadbury reacted by making their bars thinner. The shape of a piece of chocolate affects its taste, or certainly the eating experience. Yorkie was released as a small bar that actually had traditional chunks of chocolate.

7   See <www.youtube.com/watch?v=olI5xzshtFQ> and <www.youtube.com/watch?v=cDnQA583zow>.

Women and children

Table 5.4 shows that, like other categories, there is little difference in the user profile for different credit cards. But one financial institution said, 'Our brand is different', and they seemed to have a case. This Australian credit card gives a small donation to a local maternity hospital for every dollar that users spend on the card. It even features a picture of a baby on the card itself.

It is obvious that this card would have a customer base skewed towards women. Not just because the card would appeal to women but also because it wouldn't appeal to groups like young men (and maybe even young women). The marketing department told us this must be the case. But then the data came in (see Table 5.7). Cardholders are ever slightly more likely to be female than non-cardholders; but they are also more likely to be single and no more likely to have children. It appears that you don't have to be a Mum to value this credit card.

Table 5.7: Cardholds versus non-cardholders

	Male (%)	Female (%)	Single (%)	Couple with no kids (%)	Family with kids (%)	Other (%)
Cardholders	37	63	15	32	52	1
Non-cardholder customers	42	58	12	34	53	1

Source: A telephone survey based on customer lists provided by the credit card provider; see Sharp, Tolo & Giannopoulos, 2001.

I love my Mum (and you love yours)

What about differences in how a brand's buyers perceive the world? As previously explained, a brand's buyers hold the same values as buyers of other brands (see Table 5.8); but what about the buyer's attitudes towards your brand?

Table 5.8: Percentage point deviations from the brand norm: values held by brand users

Credit card brand	Children should express themselves freely	I am happy with my standard of living	I can't bear untidiness	I try to keep up with technology	I always look for special offers
Barclaycard Visa	0	–1	0	0	–1
TSB Trust card	0	–2	2	–4	2
Access Natwest	1	0	1	0	–2
Access Midlands	–1	0	1	0	–3
Access Lloyds	1	1	1	1	1
Bank of Scotland Visa	2	2	0	2	–2

Source: Adapted from Kennedy & Ehrenberg, 2000.

There is one obvious way that buyers of one brand vary from another: their brand buying. This affects their attitude to brands and their brand knowledge. People tend to have opinions about the brands they buy, and not think or know much about brands they don't use. Behaviour is a powerful driver of awareness, perceptions and attitudes.[8]

Attitudes reflect how much a buyer buys the brand, i.e. they reflect loyalty. We know that loyalty metrics don't vary a lot between brands. Consequently, the buyers of brand A have the same opinion of brand A as buyers of brand B have of brand B. I call this the 'my Mum' phenomenon:

---

8   Many research companies offer proprietary products that measure attitudinal constructs that they claim cause, and can predict, behaviour change. To prove it they report correlations with behavioural measures like loyalty or market share. These causal predictive claims are largely nonsense: the correlations simply reflect that people have attitudes and more knowledge about brands they buy (i.e. behaviour is a powerful driver of attitudes).

my own mother is the best mum in the world, she's lovely, but she can also be rather annoying sometimes. Does that sound like your mum?

Another lovely example of this was a global survey of tourists conducted by the Ehrenberg-Bass Institute. The survey asked the tourists to describe why they chose their last holiday destination. The open-ended, qualitative responses were collated for each destination; unexpectedly, the researchers noticed a high degree of similarity in the responses for each destination, for example:

- somewhere new and exciting
- interesting people and culture
- nice shopping
- somewhere to relax.

Obviously people did not talk about the snow if they went to a beach location, or the surf if they went to a mountain. But aside from these descriptive differences, the tourists' stated motivations and benefits were uncannily similar. This is another way that a brand's customer base is similar to that of other brands.

Different variants

Brand managers often add variants—also known as stock-keeping units (SKU)—to their brand in the belief that this allows the brand to reach different buyers. Let's look at variants. They are interesting because their clear functional differences could mean they are used by different people.

Table 5.9 shows the normal market shares for regular (63% share) and diet/no sugar (35% share) soft drinks, and then their market shares in particular demographic groups.[9] This sort of analysis, popular in market research reports (where indices are often used) can exaggerate differences in that it is possible to have an unusually high share, but in a tiny demographic group, so that your overall customer base isn't much

---

9   Source: TNS; data analysis by Giang Trinh, Ehrenberg-Bass Institute.

different. I've deliberately chosen this style of analysis to show even tiny potential differences, but as you can see there isn't much to show. Read the table downwards for each variant. Regular soft drink has an overall share of about two–thirds—it also has this share in each demographic. Diet soft drink has a share of about one-third, both overall and also in each demographic sub-group. So neither variant especially appeals to any particular segment (and that's in spite of years of diet soft drink advertising trying to target women).[10]

Table 5.9: Gender profile of different types of soft drink

Market share in a particular demo group	Regular soft drink (%)	Diet soft drink (%)
Overall market	63	35
Male	66	33
Female	60	37
1 person household	60	38
3+ person household	64	34
Children in household	65	32
No children in household	61	38
<34 years old	74	24
55–74 years old	59	38
AB socioeconomic	59	38
E socioeconomic	66	32

---

10 Fortunately for marketers, most targeting attempts fail because media are far less targeted than they claim. The danger is that in the future truly targeted media strategies may become available, then there is a real potential for marketers to do damage to their brands through following textbook targeting recommendations.

Now let's look at pack sizes (see Table 5.10). The large can/bottle has double the market share of the small can/bottle. This is the case in every demographic group, except among older people where small bottles are slightly less popular.

Table 5.10: Demographic profile of small versus large sized soft drink bottles

Market share in a particular demo group	Small bottle (%)	Large bottle (%)
Overall market	19	43
Male	25	38
Female	14	47
1 person household	22	44
3+ person household	20	41
Children in household	20	39
No children in household	17	46
<34 years old	37	23
55–74 years old	12	52
AB socioeconomic	17	46
E socioeconomic	17	47

Now let's compare cola with lemonade (see Table 5.11). We can see that lemonade brands do better with older buyers. But since 54–74-year-olds make up a small part of the overall market for soft drinks this skew does practically nothing to make lemonade's customer base different from cola's customer base.

It's a common assumption that product variants are developed for particular types of buyers. For example, low-allergy fabric conditioner must sell to people who suffer from allergies. In which case, if we examined

Table 5.11: Demographic profile of colas versus lemonade

Market share in a particular demo group	Cola (%)	Lemonade (%)
Overall market	40	13
Male	44	11
Female	37	14
1 person household	41	19
3+ person household	41	11
Children in household	39	10
No children in household	41	15
<34 years old	45	5
55–74 years old	34	21
AB socioeconomic	35	13
E socioeconomic	41	12

such variants we would see 'niche-type' patterns: such products would sell to a small group of highly loyal buyers. Yet generally this is not what happens. To use the specific example of (no fragrance, no colour) low-allergy fabric conditioners: these are not big sellers and they sell to a few buyers who only occasionally buy them (double jeopardy; see Chapter 2). Their loyalty metrics are barely higher than they should be as predicted by the double jeopardy law.

What this means is that low-allergy fabric conditioners mainly sell to normal fabric conditioner buyers who occasionally feel allergic (or at least think about it). There will be a few allergy sufferers who only buy low-allergy fabric conditioners, but these few 'loyalists' make up a small part of the variant's customer base.

Table 5.12: Double jeopardy law—types of fabric conditioner, US

Fabric conditioner variants	Market share (%)	Penetration (annual) (%)	Loyalty-related metrics	
			Purchase frequency (average)	Share of category requirements (%)
Regular	72	63	5.0	74
Light	20	32	3.0	33
Unscented	*4*	*9*	*2.0*	*28*
Stainguard	3	9	1.7	19
Average			2.9	39

Source: IRI; Singh, Goodhardt & Ehrenberg, 2001; Singh, Ehrenberg & Goodhardt, 2008.

Implications

The big discovery is that the customer bases of brands in a category are very similar—except in numbers of buyers. One way of thinking about it is that there isn't a vanilla ice-cream buyer and a different type of person who buys strawberry—there are just ice-cream buyers who sometimes buy vanilla and very occasionally buy strawberry.

When market research shows that a brand is selling to a different customer profile than competitor brands it's common practice for marketers to say, 'We skew towards young women, so that's our media target.' But this thinking is incorrect. What you should be saying is, 'Why?' Is there something wrong with our marketing? Are we failing to reach some demographics (and therefore overweighting in others)? It's wrong to assume that a brand appeals to a particular type of buyer; most don't and they shouldn't want to. A brand may sell to an unusual customer profile (more of some people and less of others) because it is currently marketed that way, or because of history or mistakes. None of which means that it will sell best if targeted to this audience.

A skew from the category norm needs to be checked carefully. The question is whether to market in line with this skew or to go with the category norm. Usually the answer will be the latter.

Of course, there are some expected differences, such as sugary breakfast cereal brands eaten more by children, and expensive products selling to wealthier people (who have sufficient funds to buy them). But within these sub-markets there is little difference between brand's user bases; for example, Versace sells to the same wealthier buyers as Gucci does.[11]

This is a very positive finding. It means that your brand is unrestrained, in the sense that it can grow its customer base. Because the buyers of other brands are just like your customers—they potentially could be yours. If your buyers were really different from buyers of other brands that would suggest that your brand was suited to a particular type of buyer and not others. That would suggest that you had filled your niche—time for the marketing department to all go home.

But your niche appears to be the whole market, so there is plenty of growth potential. All that is standing in your way is a degree of brand loyalty, and the fact that you have competitors with similar growth aspirations. Of course, this implication also works in reverse. Your competitors see that your customers are just like theirs, so there is nothing structural preventing them from stealing your customers. This is another reason why it's not time for the marketing department to go home.

Given how stark this finding is, and how readily available customer profile data is, it seems odd that this discovery is a surprise to many marketers.[12] Perhaps it is due to us expecting to see differences. Marketing textbooks tell us that brands have been differentiated and targeted to specific segments. Therefore we expect them to sell to different sorts of

---

11   However, Gucci has many more buyers, far greater sales revenue and lots more stores (see Chapter 12).

12   Researchers newly recruited to the Ehrenberg-Bass Institute, and marketing executives from our corporate sponsors, regularly report that this finding is very surprising. The conference paper by Kennedy & Ehrenberg won two awards for its implications.

customers. Also, many marketing directors find that they have a large portfolio of brands, many inherited in historic company acquisitions. They look for a reason why they have all these very similar brands and conclude that each must appeal to different sorts of buyers, whereas in reality they appeal to different buyers, but not different types of buyers, i.e. they appeal to the particular buyers that know them.

Competition

The very good news is that there is nothing structural standing in the way of your brand growing; your competitor's customers could be yours. The only problem is that you have competitors who are trying to do the same as you. Therefore, brands need capable marketing departments to defend them.

What then do these marketing laws mean for competition? Does a brand compete with all other brands in its category? How does a brand identify its nearest competitors? This is the topic of the next chapter.

Who Do You Really Compete With?

Byron Sharp

In Chapter 4 I suggested that textbooks have condemned mass market-ing to a premature grave. This is what Philip Kotler and colleagues (1998) have written about mass marketing and how brands compete with one another:

> Marketing has passed through three stages:
>
> 1 **Mass marketing.** [Here] the seller mass produces, mass distributes and mass promotes one product to all buyers. At one time, Coca-Cola produced only one drink for the whole market, hoping it would appeal to everyone. The argument for mass marketing is that it should lead to the lowest costs and prices and create the largest potential market.
>
> 2 **Product-variety marketing**. Here, the seller produces two or more products that have different features, styles, quality, sizes and so on. Later, Coca-Cola produced several soft drinks packaged in different sizes and containers. They were designed to offer variety to buyers rather than to appeal to different segments. The argument for product-variety marketing is that consumers have different tastes that change over time. Consumers seek variety and change.

3   **Target marketing.** Here, the seller identifies market segments, selects one or more of them, and develops products and marketing mixes tailored to each. For example, Coca-Cola now produces soft drinks for the sugared-cola segment, the diet segment, the no-caffeine segment and the non-cola segment.

Sellers can develop the right product for each target market and adjust their prices, distribution channels and advertising to reach the target market efficiently. Instead of scattering their marketing efforts (the 'shotgun' approach), they can focus on the buyers who have greater purchase interest (the 'rifle' approach).

Source: Kotler et al., 1998.

According to Kotler and colleagues (1998), brands are supposed to target segments of the market, which would severely limit the number of other brands they compete with.

While this may sound logical and straightforward, there are a number of problems with this theory. It's difficult to think of a real-world example of mass marketing that fits the extreme definition: few, if any, firms have only one product, with one price. It is also unclear how the examples of target marketing differ from the less sophisticated 'product-variety marketing'. Yes, Coca-Cola now markets many brands of soft drink, but is this to satisfy the distinct needs of particular groups of buyers, or to satisfy individuals' demand for variety, or a bit of both? Oddly, according to Kotler, offering containers of different sizes caters for variety seeking, but different flavours cater for different people!

Simply naming a segment does not make it exist. We could similarly create 'segment' names to match Kotler's product-variety strategy (e.g. the high quality seeking segment, the large pack economy oriented segment, and so on). However, for this to have any meaning there would need to be empirical evidence that each of Coca-Cola's brands really does sell to different people. Kotler presents no such data to ground his claims.

Table 6.1 shows that various soft drink brands share their customer base with Coca-Cola; that is, the table shows what proportion of each soft drink brand's customers also bought Coca-Cola during the analysis period. The data is from the TNS Impulse Panel (UK), which I have specifically chosen because it covers individual consumers buying for their personal use. Therefore, the repertoire of brand buying shown in the table is not due to different brands being bought by different people in the same household.

Table 6.1: Sharing of customers

Buyers of X during the analysis period	Percentage of X buyers who also bought (regular) Coca-Cola during the period
Diet Coke	65
Fanta	70
Lilt	67
Pepsi	72
Average	**69**

Source: TNS.

As you can see, a high proportion of each brand's buyers also bought Coca-Cola, and this proportion varies little between the different brands—it's always about two-thirds of their customer base.[1] This empirical evidence counters Kotler's idea that individual brands sell to distinctly different segments of buyers—brands share customers. Several of the brands are even marketed by the Coca-Cola company—these brands share their customers with Coca-Cola as much as rival company's brands do.

Customer-sharing data gives insight into who competes against who. If brands are close rivals, then they should be in the repertoires of the same people, i.e. they share customers.[2] Logically, brands that are direct

---

1 Of course, the actual *number* of customers shared with Coca-Cola depends on the size of the brand and on how many customers they have to share.

2 If they are complementary products (e.g. taco shells and refried beans) then we'd expect high levels of sharing. But complementary products are easy to identify prior to any customer-sharing analysis. Brands within a product/service category are nearly always rivals not complementary. They share customers because they compete with one another as alternatives.

competitors within a product category should show higher levels of sharing, and brands that target different segments should share fewer customers.

Duplication of purchase analysis

The extraordinary fact about the sharing analysis is not that Pepsi buyers also buy Coca-Cola (although this surprises some people), but that each brand shares a near identical proportion of its customer base with Coca-Cola.

The exact degree of sharing depends on the period of analysis. If it is long enough, then nearly all of a brand's customers will have also bought Coca-Cola, whereas over a very short time period a smaller proportion a brand's customers will have also bought Coca-Cola. However, the length of time affects all brands equally, so it doesn't affect inter-brand comparisons. Irrespective of the time period, each brand of soft drink shares a similar proportion of its consumers with Coca-Cola.

This suggests that all the brands compete *equally closely* with Coca-Cola, and that none of them sell to special discrete segments of buyers. Perhaps this is because Coca-Cola is so large. Perhaps no soft drink brand can get away from competing with Coke. But how do brands compete with less ubiquitous brands? Let's now expand the analysis to consider all brands in a category.

A 'duplication of purchase' table[3] shows the degree to which brands within a category share their buyers with each of the other brands in the category, i.e. what proportion of their customers also bought another particular brand during the period. Table 6.2 is a duplication of purchase table with no data.

---

3   Also sometimes called a brand-switching table, but the term switching is clumsy, as it implies defection from one brand and uptake of a new (to the buyer) brand, which is an exaggeration. Just because I bought Fanta this time when I more often buy Coke doesn't mean anything has changed about my Coca-Cola buying; I just occasionally buy Fanta. Duplication of purchase tables reflect how people hold repertoires of brands, i.e. divided polygamous loyalty.

Table 6.2: Duplication of purchase

Buyers of brand	Percentage of buyers who also bought brand			
	A	B	C	D
A	100%			
B		100%		
C			100%	
D				100%

The 100% cells are a brand's level of customer overlap with itself, which logically must always be 100%. In terms of the presentation of the data, it's good practice to blank out these cells because they are not needed.

Duplication of purchase tables refer to a particular time period, for example, the people during the year who bought brand A who also bought brand B. Note that a buyer of brand A needs to only make one purchase of brand B to be counted. Consequently, duplication analyses that apply to very long periods can be misleading, because every brand may show very high levels of sharing with every other brand, which obscures who competes more or less closely. At the other end of the time spectrum, in very short time periods there is often no duplication (because many customers have only bought the category once), which is also misleading. The analyst should choose a period long enough to capture a degree of repeated purchase, i.e. a period long enough to allow most people to have bought multiple brands. Readers of duplication tables need to note that they refer to a particular period, there is never an absolute metric; one can't simply say, '70% of Pepsi buyers drink Coke'—it's 70% *in a year*.

The duplication of purchase law

Let's look at a duplication of purchase table for ice-cream brands (see Table 6.3).

Table 6.3: Duplication of purchase—ice-cream, 2005

	Percentage of buyers who also bought brand						
Buyers of brand	Walls Carte D'Or	Walls Dessert	Ben & Jerry's	Häagen Dazs	Nestlé	Walls	Mars
(Walls) Carte D'Or	–	15	8	8	9	5	4
Walls Dessert	34	–	7	8	9	4	3
Ben & Jerry's	38	14	–	26	13	7	8
Häagen Dazs	37	17	26	–	8	7	8
Nestlé	39	17	12	7	–	8	9
Walls	37	14	12	11	15	–	11
Mars	41	12	18	17	22	13	–
Average	**38**	**15**	**14**	**13**	**13**	**7**	**7**

Source: TNS.

There are three striking patterns in the above table:

1 Every brand shares much more of its customer base with the largest brand, Carte D'Or, than with Mars, the brand with the smallest market share.
2 There is similarity in the degree of sharing with any particular brand. For example, *all* brands share 40% of their customers (+ or – only a few percentage points) with Carte D'Or during the period of analysis.
3 There are a few deviations to the above two patterns. For example, Ben & Jerry's shares more than expected with Häagen Dazs.

The first two patterns reflect what is known as the duplication of purchase law. This law says that *all brands, within a category, share their customer base with other brands in line with the size of those other brands*. In other words, everyone shares a lot with big brands and a little with small brands.

The duplication of purchase law would not hold if several brands successfully targeted exclusive customer bases, or particular types of people who are different from the buyers of other brands.[4] However, as we saw in Chapter 5, rival brands sell to very similar customer bases.

In Table 6.3 the brands are ranked in market share order, both across columns and rows, so you can easily see that duplication of customers declines in line with this rank. Every brand shares most with Carte D'Or because it is the largest brand—it has about three times the penetration of most of the other brands in the table.

Armed with knowledge of the duplication of purchase law, it is possible to spot market partitions: clusters of brands whose customer bases overlap more than expected. The law can also be used to spot brands that show unusually low overlap in their customer bases.

The ice-cream buying data covers premium and not-so-premium brands, brands only sold in large tubs and brands only sold as bars/cones. This affects their distribution, as some outlets only stock large tubs and some only stock small bars/cones. Given these notable functional differences we should expect a partitioned market. The real surprise is how unpartitioned it is; in order words, the market is not far off being one mass market. Now that is an insight.

The only obvious partition is Ben & Jerry's and Häagen Dazs sharing with each other almost double the amount of customers that they share with other brands; though it is worth observing that Ben & Jerry's customers are still more likely to buy Carte D'Or than Häagen Dazs. However, the duplication of purchase law has been bent a little rather, than broken.

Marketers often fall into the trap of underestimating how broadly their brand really competes. Segmentation studies overstate very small differences, and it's assumed that brands with different features (e.g. price

---

4   Some brands might successfully target a particular usage or occasion rather than type of person, for example, ice-creams to eat at the movies. Yet this still might be expected to produce demographic differences in customer bases, and deviations from the duplication of purchase law.

levels) must sell to very different people, or for very different buying situations. These assumptions are often unrealistic or exaggerated. It is useful to start the duplication of purchase analysis with a very broad market definition, then if partitions appear, undertake separate duplication analyses, for example, a separate premium ice-cream category and an everyday ice-cream category.

Potential uses

The duplication of purchase law can be used to find partitions and, therefore, to understand the structure of a market. The law can provide a consumer-buying based guide to define the product category. This can be extremely useful, if only to reduce the debates between managers about category definition. Importantly, it can help prevent the blinkered, production-oriented vision that comes from category definitions based on product features or production processes. These are rife, and are typically too narrow. For example, the chocolate market can be divided into dozens of sub-markets (block, bars, pieces, individually wrapped, candy coated, chocolate coated candy, and so on). These product-based category definitions can blind managers to their true competitors and prevent them from understanding how customers actually buy.

Ehrenberg-Bass Institute researcher John Bound tells a lovely story about when he was a market research manager for Quaker Oats in the UK. At the time research suppliers thought there was a hot breakfast cereal category and a cold breakfast cereal category (among others). Then one day someone pointed out that the cold breakfast cereals still sold well in the middle of (a very cold English) winter. Researchers were immediately sent out into the field to investigate what was going on; they discovered the naughty consumers were putting hot milk on their cold breakfast cereal![5] This example shows that product-oriented category definitions isolate brand managers from real buying behaviour.

---

5   Consumers often behave as if they haven't read the marketing plans for the brands they buy.

Even consumption situation-based category definitions (e.g. for snacking, for sharing, for gifting) commonly result in artificial overly narrow category definitions. The reality is that few brands are exclusively bought for specific consumption situations, and which brands are bought for which situation varies between consumers and over time.

Narrow category definitions lull brand managers into a false sense of security and can result in unduly conservative growth targets. Brand managers prefer category definitions that make their brand appear to have a substantial market share—no one like to be ranked seventeenth. Therefore, narrow category definitions are commonly adopted. These also make growth potential, particularly penetration potential, appear more limited than it really is.

In addition to giving guidance regarding category definition, and showing which brands compete with which, the duplication of purchase law can also be used to predict where new brands will steal sales from (and so can estimate cannibalisation of sales of sister brands). This is essential for planning the launch of a new product.

The duplication of purchase law also shows up in customer defection and acquisition. A brand will gain most of its new customers from the largest brands, and will also lose more of its customers to larger brands. Therefore, the law can be used as benchmark for customer defection and acquisition to and from each of a brand's competitors. For example, if a brand is losing more customers to another brand than you would expect given that brand's size, then this indicates some unusual overlap in marketing strategy. (Perhaps the competing brand has opened a store close by?)

Marketing strategy insight

Duplication of purchase analysis does more than show who competes against whom. The fact that there is such a natural law (that describes sharing in most categories rather well) tells us about how brands compete in general. We live and work in a world of mass markets. Ben & Jerry's and Häagen Dazs, while they are close competitors, also compete against all other ice-cream brands, especially large ones like Carte D'Or. Such patterns hold around the world and in different product/service categories. For example, customer gains for BMW in France come more from large non-premium brands like Renault, Citroën and Peugeot than from smaller luxury brands like Mercedes and Audi (Ehrenberg, 1999).

Partitions exist in markets; premium quality/price partitions are particularly common. But it is sensible to think of these divisions as sub-markets (partitions) rather than as entirely separate markets.

Positioning and partitioning

This story of customer overlap is at odds with the picture provided by perceptual maps (and other brand image analyses). This picture is usually of some brands competing closely with each other, and very indirectly with other brands in the competitive set; a typical perceptual map might look like Figure 6.1 (the brands are marked in circles).

Figure 6.1: Perceptual map—flavoured milk

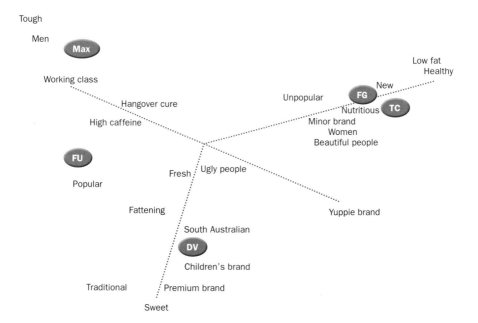

This perceptual map for flavoured milk (iced coffee) in Australia implies there are very significant market partitions. The brand Max is for working-class males; Farmers' Union is mainstream and devoid of a brand 'image'; Dairy Vale is a children's brand, or perhaps is sweet and luxurious; while Feel Good and Take Care are new, healthy brands for women. However, duplication of purchase analyses have shown that market partitions are generally due to substantial functional differences and similarities between brands, factors like where or when they are physically available, rather than their brand images.

Table 6.4 is a duplication of purchase analysis for the same flavoured milk brands based on the actual buying of the same consumers who provided the data for the perceptual map.

Table 6.4: Duplication of purchase—flavoured milk

Buyers of brand	Percentage of buyers who also bought brand				
	Farmers' Union	Dairy Vale	Take Care	Max	Feel Good
Farmers' Union		21	8	6	5
Dairy Vale	43		5	5	5
Take Care	52	16		0	20
Max	45	20	0		0
Feel Good	53	27	33	0	
Average	48	21	12	3	8

Source: Sharp, Sharp & Redford, 2003.

The main evident pattern is the duplication of purchase law. The brands are ordered according to market share and it is easy to see that every brand shares about half their customers, during this period, with the largest brand: Farmers' Union. There is very little customer overlap with the smallest brands: Max and Feel Good.

As far as evident market partitions, there is one clear partition involving Take Care and Feel Good. These brands share customers to a far higher degree than the duplication of purchase law would predict (see the numbers in bold in Table 6.4). The Take Care and Feel Good products both have zero sugar and low fat—as suggested by their names. These functional differences show up both in duplication of purchase and in the perceptual map.

The perceptual map correctly shows that Take Care and Feel Good are close competitors, but it exaggerates the degree to which these brands are isolated from competition from the other brands. Both these brands still share more customers with the large brand Farmers' Union than they do with each other—many consumers buy both. In general, perceptual maps often suggest more market segmentation than really exists (Sharp, 1997b). This is partly due to the underlying statistical methods, which are designed to highlight differences; these methods are also sensitive to outliers in the data set.

Implications for brand portfolio management

Should marketers worry if their company has several similar brands? Should these brands be collapsed together, should some be dropped, or should marketers strive to position them differently? In general, the answer is don't worry.

Companies often have similar brands that sell to similar populations. Coke has Diet Coke and Coke Zero (and Regular Coke). Mars have the Mars Bar and Snickers. P&G has Tampax and Always. General Motors has Saturn Astra and Chevy Aveo. This isn't something to worry about. It's normal for brands in a category to compete against one another and to sell to near identical customer bases. Even brands that are obviously quite different (e.g. KFC and McDonalds, Visa and AmEx) still directly compete.

Heinz doesn't worry that it offers tomato soup as well as vegetable soup. Similarly a marketer shouldn't worry about their company having similar brands. If a new soft drink company could choose to own and market any two global brands, should it choose Coke and Fanta? No, it should choose Coke and Pepsi, because these are the biggest brands globally, with the most valuable market-based assets.

What marketers should worry about is whether or not their brands are distinctive. Are they easy to recognise and distinguish from others? If they are not, the brand's advertising won't work—and consumers won't see the product on the shelf. So brands should look different (this is what branding is about) even if they don't compete as differentiated brands (see Chapter 8).

Marketers should also worry about the total portfolio effects of price promotions. When one of a company's brands is on special, this not only takes full-priced sales that would have happened anyway, it also steals full-priced sales from the company's other brands.

If brands grow they will always steal from the other brands in the same product category. The exact amount of cannibalisation that will occur between brands can be predicted by the duplication of purchase law. What you need to watch out for is excessive cannibalisation. Companies tend to be good at stealing sales from themselves because their brands go through the same sales force, the same distributors, etc. Marketers need to acknowledge and accept this, but to also be on the look-out for excessive cannibalisation.

Finally, the decision to drop, phase out or sell brands should be based on viability, cost and operating issues and not on how similar the brand is to another of the company's brands. This is especially true if the brands are well established with substantial market-based assets.

Modern sophisticated mass marketing

Markets are usually a little fragmented, but within common-sense definitions they still largely function as mass markets. The small degree of fragmentation is often catered for by brand variants,[6] which leaves

---

6   We saw in Chapter 5 that even brand variants (SKUs) largely sell to similar customer bases.

marketers still needing to know how to compete in a mass market. This is Kotler's 'product variety marketing', which is a type of mass marketing.

Toothpaste is often used as an example of segment marketing where marketers have broken the market into many sub-markets. For example, Colgate provides numerous varieties, each of which is supposed to successfully target and meet the needs of specific consumers. 'These include "normal" toothpaste, gel toothpaste, children's toothpaste, tooth whitening toothpastes, anti-bacterial, tartar control, toothpaste for sensitive teeth, and toothpaste with extra strong fluoride' (Kotler et al., 1998). However, there is little evidence that Colgate actually *targets* specific market segments. To say there is a tartar control segment as evidenced by the tartar control toothpaste is circular logic. Kotler and colleagues (1998, p. 296) tell us that segment marketers 'develop the right product for each target market and adjust their prices, distribution channels and advertising to reach the target market efficiently'. But this does not hold up to scrutiny in the Colgate example (and for Coca-Cola discussed earlier). Colgate does not use different distribution channels for their tartar control product. In fact their products are all on the same shelf, in the same stores, put there by the same merchandisers. The products' prices are often within cents of one another and, while there might be different ads for some products (alongside much corporate brand advertising), these ads typically appear in the same (mass) media—television ads in particular are known for their wide, unsegmented reach. The difference in each product's marketing mix is limited to the difference that exists between each product variant. The role of advertising is only to 'bring to public notice' that different products exist and are available. These marketing practices fit perfectly Kotler's definition of mass, product-variety marketing—which is exactly the marketing situation that most firms find themselves in.

Therefore, brand managers need to be cognisant of *all* their competitors. They should be wary of thinking that their brand is partitioned or positioned away from other brands. It might be fashionable for a brand manager to call him- or herself a target marketer, but it's best to think like a sophisticated mass marketer. This means being aware of the considerable heterogeneity within the mass market; for example, in purchase frequency and in the brands that individuals buy. Within the mass market there are lots of different buyers. Sophisticated mass marketers cleverly react to this heterogeneity (e.g. by marketing multiple brands and variants, by using multiple media and distribution channels), and rather than trying to hem their brands into niches, they are always looking for avenues for broad reach.

Passionate Consumer Commitment

Byron Sharp

Are buyers puppets?

Nike is routinely held up as a super brand, but its sales and style are similar to Adidas. The sportswear market has a plethora of similar competing brands (Reebok, Puma, New Balance and Coq Sportif);[1] one explanation for this brand proliferation is that marketers have used advertising and packaging to fool buyers into adopting irrational preferences and loyalties. This explanation has been put forward by both opponents and advocates of advertising and branding. There are plenty of psychological studies that support this argument, but they also suggest advertising and packaging has a very weak psychological effect (even under laboratory conditions).

Two recent, widely reported (and misreported) psychological studies are typical. Each purports to show that branding can distort preferences. In one study (McClure et al., 2004), 67 volunteers were given brain scans

---

1   All these brands have benefited from the growth of the sports wear category; this growth was due to sports wear becoming street wear.

while tasting tiny squirts of cola dispensed via a plastic tube. Subjects also undertook more traditional, though still artificial, taste tests (i.e. sips out of little cups). Also, 16 of the subjects undertook blind taste tests and about half chose Pepsi and half chose Coke. Their choice in the blind tests poorly correlated with the preference they stated prior to the test: about the same number of those who had stated they preferred Coke chose Pepsi in the blind trial, and about the same number of subjects who preferred Pepsi chose Coke. Other subjects were again each given two samples of the same cola. One sample was identified as either Coke or Pepsi, while the brand of the other sample was not revealed—subjects were told that the second unidentified cola could be either Coke or Pepsi (though in reality it was always the same cola as the first sample).[2]

When the labelled cola was Coke, subjects largely said it tasted best. The same did not occur when Pepsi was the identified cola. This may have been due to the groups consisting of more people who usually tend to drink Coca-Cola (in this case prior preferences were not checked).

Then all the subjects were given MRI brain scans while being given computer-administered squirts of cola through plastic tubes. They were not asked to express a preference. The main finding was that when subjects were told that Coke was the cola they were sipping more brain activity was recorded in the hippocampus and in other brain areas thought to be concerned with cultural knowledge and memories. This did not occur quite so much for Pepsi.

What does this tell us? First, in artificial tasting situations people are far more likely to trust their eyes than their sense of taste. They also react as if it were a test—that their performance is being judged, not just the colas. So informing them that one cup contains their favourite cola (or non-favourite cola) largely over-rides their taste buds—which is especially

---

2   It is often said that this experiment is based on the Pepsi challenge. However, the famous Pepsi challenge consists of two unlabelled cups, one containing Pepsi and one Coke, which differs from this experiment where both cups contain the same cola. With both cups containing the same cola, respondents obviously found it hard to detect a difference and so were probably easily swayed by the label.

easy when the other cup contains the same cola (i.e. there is no difference between the two cups). This phenomenon has been observed across decades of taste testing research. Second, the brain scans probably reflect something that psychologists have known for decades: familiarity breeds liking. Usage also breeds familiarity and brand knowledge; this in turn breeds liking.

This is very much what the second recent, widely reported study shows. In this research (Robinson et al., 2007), 63 children aged between three and five years old were given two identical food items to taste. One item was in plain wrapping and the other was in McDonald's branded wrapping. The food items were McDonald's hamburgers, chicken McNuggets, McDonald's French fries, milk and two baby carrots. With each exposure of a food item, for example, McDonald's French fries, the child was asked, 'Can you tell me which of these foods is from McDonald's?' If the child did not answer or answered incorrectly the administrator pointed to the McDonald's branded option and said, 'This food is from McDonald's'; this happened about a third of the time. Each child was then instructed to take a bite of each of the two options and the administrator then asked, 'Tell me if they taste the same or point to the food [drink] that tastes best to you'. The children chose the branded option (as tasting best) 182 times. 122 times they chose the unbranded option or said they both tasted the same (or that they did not know).

The more regularly a child ate at McDonald's (as reported by their parents), the more likely they were to choose the branded item.[3] Also, children with more television sets in their home were also more likely to select the branded item. But other moderator variables—having a television in the bedroom, having McDonald's toys in the house, and hours of television viewing—had no detectable influence.

Decades of testing preferences and quality cues has taught us that when a single cue is introduced into a study respondents react strongly to it. This is probably because subjects feel they are supposed to react to the cue.

---

3   Only two children had never eaten McDonald's, and about a third ate McDonald's weekly or more regularly (as reported by their parents).

However, because it is the only cue, it becomes artificially salient. It is surprising that these sorts of artificial studies are still being done. Similar weak preferential results might probably be gained by simply wrapping one of the items in coloured paper and the other in plain.

Therefore, we shouldn't read too much into these sorts of studies, which very often have a political agenda behind them. They invariably find results in the direction the researchers expected. What is worth noting is how mild the effects are, even in these artificial constructions. The main finding again seems to be that prior usage of the brand makes a person slightly more favourable towards it. This is one of the psychological factors underpinning brand loyalty.

Brand loyalty—a natural part of buying behaviour

Brand loyalty is part of every market, even in so called commodity categories. Rather than thinking of loyalty as a market imperfection, it is more appropriately considered to be a sensible buyer strategy, one of many developed by human beings in order to balance risk and avoid wasting the precious commodity of time.

In 1964 Professor Tucker of Texas University conducted an interesting experiment into the development of brand loyalty. His experiment revealed that buyers naturally tend towards brand loyalty—loyalty is a buying strategy that most of us adopt much of the time. In Tucker's experiment, each day, for 12 days, loaves of bread from the same commercial oven were offered on a tray for choice to 42 women. The loaves were wrapped identically, and each day one was labelled L, another M, P and H. The position of the brands on the tray was rotated. In spite of the loaves being identical, many of the respondents quickly adopted loyal behaviours, with each woman favouring a particular brand. Some also favoured positions on the tray (e.g. tending to choose the brand that was on the left of the tray). This landmark study concluded that it is clear that brand loyalty is based on what may seem to be trivial distinctions.

However, Tucker's study was limited and somewhat artificial. It could be argued that buyers are used to more substantial differences in real-world brands and so acted as if there might be in this study. Also, tastes vary day by day, and maybe the bread varied too—if one day a loaf didn't taste so good to a subject perhaps she avoided that brand on the following days. Even so, the study did show that consumers have a predilection to adopt loyalty behaviours, for whatever reason. This is further evidenced by the fact that brand loyalty is a characteristic of every market.

In Chapter 3 we saw that repeat-purchasing levels for car brands are quite high, i.e. around 50% repeat levels (with some variation between countries); almost half the time new car buyers buy the same brand as they bought last time. This level of repeat-buying seems incredible considering that in modern market economies there are typically 60 or so brands to choose from. Also, usually a number of years pass between purchases, models change, as do buyer's life circumstances and needs. The odds of someone choosing the same car brand again appears to be very slim. If buying were random, there would be less than 1 chance in 50 of a person purchasing the same brand again. But buying is not random; there is clear behavioural preference and loyalty.

We observe this sort of loyalty in all categories, including service categories and corporate buying. Buyers restrict their purchases to a personal repertoire of brands. People buy far fewer different brands than they could. 10 purchases seldom results in 10 different brands being bought. Buyers keep returning to their favourites,[4] and this set of favourites can be very small. The 50% repeat-buying rate for car brands occurs because buyers consider only around two brands on average, one of which is usually the brand they bought last time (i.e. the brand they drive now) (Lambert-Pandraud, 2005). About a fifth of buyers consider only a single brand, which is almost always the one they bought last (Lapersonne, 1995). (Yet this is what buyer behaviour texts refer to as a 'highly involving purchase decision'!)

---

4   I use the term 'favourites' with some caution as it implies that buyers have strong attitudinal preferences, which often simply isn't the case. I'm using this term to refer to the fact that we have brands that we favour (i.e our repeat purchasing is biased towards these brands).

Here's another surprising example. The choice of which television channel to watch is a category where loyalty is unexpected. Most of us think we watch television for the programs, and, aside from the genre-specific channels (e.g. the weather channel), we have only a vague idea of what channel offers our favourite programs. Also, there are no real switching costs: we can defect from one channel by pushing a button. In spite of all this, television channel choice shows the same pattern as other categories—people substantially restrict their repertoires and show loyalty.

Figure 7.1 was compiled by Ehrenberg-Bass Institute researcher Virginia Beal; it is based on Nielsen data on US households in 2002. The figure shows the number of television channels each household has access to in their subscription and how many they actually watch. The key point is how quickly the line flattens; when a household has access to 40 channels they watch about a dozen or so each week, households with access to 80 channels watch a few more than a dozen each week, and

Figure 7.1: Number of television channels watched in US households, 2002

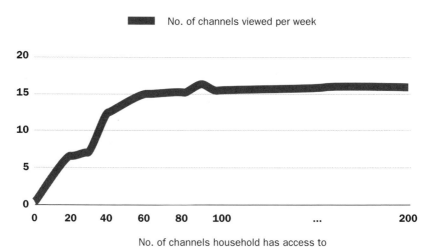

Source: Virginia Beal, Nielsen.

households with access to 200 channels still only watch a few more than a dozen each week.

What Figure 7.1 shows is that viewers (sensibly) keep returning to their favourite channels. There is obvious loyalty. Most viewers watch enough television to watch many more channels than they do, but they prefer to restrict their personal repertoire. Figure 7.1 would look almost identical if it examined brand buying in any category, for example, if it instead showed the number of purchases made by an individual and how many different brands they had bought. Loyalty is everywhere, from soap to soap operas.

Divided loyalty

Universal loyalty is not exclusive—buyers purchase more than one brand, and the more purchases an individual makes the more brands he or she buys. Polygamous or divided loyalty is quite the norm. So no brand should expect its buyers to be 100% loyal.

Table 7.1 lists the proportion of a brand's buyers who were exclusively loyal to that brand (in a particular year). The average for this selection of brands is 13% of their buyer base. The double jeopardy law holds again for this loyalty metric: smaller brands have a smaller proportion of their customer base who are 100% loyal. All these brands are among the major brands in their respective categories—the metric is even lower for very small brands.

Notice that the categories that are purchased less frequently have higher levels of 100% loyalty. Analgesics are bought only five times a year on average, and because this is a skewed average (see Chapter 4), more than half of all households bought from the category only once. These once-only buyers, by definition, have to appear among the 100% loyal buyers—if you only buy once then you can buy only one brand. As time goes by these buyers make more purchases and the proportion that are 100% loyal drops dramatically. This can be seen in categories like breakfast cereals and yoghurts, which are bought more frequently and so show much lower levels of 100% brand loyalty.

Table 7.1: 100% loyal buyers are the minority

Product	Annual category purchase rate (average)	Brand size (market share) (%)	100% loyal buyers among brand buyers (%)
Analgesics	5.1		
	Tesco	22	37
	Nurofen	8	28
	Boots	3	26
	Panadol	2	29
Deodorants	5.6		
	Lynx	17	21
	Dove	7	17
	Tesco	4	14
	Nivea	2	10
Crisps (potato chips)	17.5		
	Walkers	68	37
	KP	7	6
	Kettle Foods	1	10
Ready-to-eat breakfast cereals	21.5		
	Kellogs	29	7
	Cereal Partners	17	2
	Weet-bix	9	2
Yoghurts	29.7		
	Muller	24	7
	Muller Light	14	4
	Ski	4	2
	Danone	3	2
Average		**13**	**13**

Source: TNS.

The standout in the above table is Walkers chips brand: a third of its buyers were exclusively loyal over the time period. Yet this level of 100% loyalty is normal for a brand with its extraordinary market share.[5] Walkers dominates the UK potato chip market, and has incredible availability; this makes it very easy for buyers to only buy Walkers—particularly if they don't make many purchases.

Natural monopoly law

Larger brands tend to have proportionately more light buyers in their user bases. Light, occasional buyers favour the bigger brands. This is purely a statistical effect and is known as the 'natural monopoly law' (i.e. larger brands have a monopoly on light buyers). For example, if you only buy one soft drink this year, then odds are it will be Coca-Cola. If you buy just one pack of crisps in the UK, then odds are it will be Walkers.

Put another way, if we observe an English person eating Walkers crisps then we know little about their buying. They are simply part of the majority of the UK population who buy Walkers at some time or another. But if we observe someone eating Red Mill[6] (a brand with 2% annual penetration) then odds are that the person is a very regular buyer of salty snacks.

The natural monopoly law is illustrated with the data in Table 7.2. Heinz buyers purchase tomato sauce four times a year, whereas buyers of C&B sauce buy tomato sauce eight times a year, i.e. twice as often[7] (though C&B is only, on average, bought for 1.2 of these eight purchases).

---

5   Remember if a brand has 100% share then all its buyers must be 100% loyal. This loyalty metric (percentage of 100% loyal buyers in the customer base) rises with market share, like all other measures of loyalty.

6   See <www.snacks.co.uk>.

7   This is an extreme example because of the extraordinary market share of Heinz, which translates to large differences in metrics between it and other brands. Normally the natural monopoly pattern is mild, particularly if the analyst is only looking at the top dozen brands. There are other categories, like television programs, where there are incredible differences in market share, and so the natural monopoly pattern is quite marked. There are some television programs that are watched by hardly anyone compared to popular shows, and these tiny programs have a viewing base substantially skewed to the heaviest of television viewers (i.e. people who watch almost everything).

Table 7.2: Smaller brands are bought by heavier category buyers

Tomato sauce (ketchup) brands	Market share (%)	Penetration (%)	Frequency of buying this brand (units per annum)	Frequency of buying any tomato sauce (units per annum)
Heinz	53	50	2.9	4
Daddies sauce	4	5	2	6
C&B sauce	1	2	1.2	8

Source: TNS.

Therefore, larger brands have more 100% loyal buyers partly because they have a lot of buyers who haven't made many purchases during the analysis period.

If we use a longer analysis period, the proportion of 100% loyal buyers always declines. Give people sufficient time to make multiple purchases and they will buy more brands.

Loyalty certainly exists, but it is tempered by opportunity. People who buy from a category less often have less opportunity to be disloyal. Similarly, people who shop from stores that stock few brands also appear more loyal (e.g. people who live in smaller towns).

Prosaic, not passionate, loyalty

So this is the everyday story of loyalty that we gain from observing people's real buying behaviour over time.[8] In the real world loyalty is everywhere, and every brand has some, but loyalty is divided and strongly driven by opportunity. This is a more prosaic picture than most marketing texts paint.

---

8   There are more exotic stories of passionate loyalty but these seldom come from observing buyers, and never from observing large number of buyers repeatedly buying. Instead, these myths originate from interrogating small samples of biased customers.

LOVEMARKS?

According to Fournier and Yao (1997), the following (paraphrased) stories show that there can be powerful bonds between consumers and brands.

Pamela: the case of falling in love

Pamela, a single mum in her 30s, is strongly attached to the brand of coffee she has bought for the past five years. Her connection is affectively laden, perhaps best compared to the notion of falling in love. The strong bond Pamela has with her coffee is at least in part rooted in its personification of special qualities that collectively build Pamela's self-worth and esteem.

While Pamela dwells on her passion for her coffee brand her intentions reveal only circumscribed commitment to the brand. Pamela is accepting of other potential brand partners. Her faithfulness lies in her emotional bond with the brand, and not in formal pledges of fidelity or anticipated future commitments. She is in love with it, not married to it.

Sara: the case of adolescent best friends

Sara is a 23-year-old mid-westerner who has recently relocated to the east coast to attend graduate school. Her coffee brand helps Sara reinforce a positive identity in a developmentally crucial time in her life. In addition to leaving the mid-western farm that defines her legacy, Sara has recently declared that she is a lesbian. In some sense, the overt self-indulgence implied in the brand helps Sara explicitly maintain her sense of self-respect in the face of social challenges to her pronouncement.

Source: Paraphrased from Fournier & Yao, 1997.

Pity the poor marketing directors. It's not enough to merely build and maintain sales and deliver profits to stockholders; they also have to get consumers to feel a deep, passionate commitment to their brand. It's no longer sufficient to have consumers who pay money to buy the brand; they have to also love the brand.

This sounds like a very tough task, yet, perversely, many marketers embrace the idea, perhaps because merely selling things sounds crass. Many marketing texts talk about creating value, delivering customer satisfaction and building relationships. This makes the marketing profession appear so much more honourable.

This current marketing orthodoxy means that it is derogatory to suggest to a brand manager that the loyalty his or her brand enjoys is due to habit, availability and/or lack of caring on behalf of buyers. Academics have long derided such buying behaviour with pernicious terms such as 'spurious loyalty'.[9] Marketing consultants and professors urge brand managers to build deep relationships with their buyers. Market researchers offer tools to find passionately loyal buyers.

Consumers can apparently even have deep attachments to cheap everyday consumer goods. In 1997 a highly respected academic journal included an article based on long (2–3.5 hours), paid interviews with eight coffee drinkers (see text box, on page 99, for a flavour of the article). The authors of the article proposed that consumers have deep and complex relationships with (coffee) brands—and their research findings turned out

---

9   There is a very long history of marketing writers debating what true loyalty is. This is a perfect example of what the twentieth century's most famous philosopher of science, Sir Karl Popper, called essentialism: seeking to define the essence of an abstract theoretical concept (Esslemont & Wright, 1994). We can all forever debate issues (like, What is true love? What is marketing?), but as these questions are about the definitions we decide to use there is no logical way of ever resolving them. To suggest that one approach captures the true meaning of brand loyalty, while another (by implication) does not, is bad philosophy, and bad science. Contrary to popular belief the purpose of science is not to say what things are but rather to say things about things: how they behave, how they relate to other things. Physicists can tell you a great deal about the properties and behaviour of things like gravity and mass while there is no set understanding of what these things are. Hence, this book is about what we can say about real world loyalty-type behaviour, both verbal behaviour (expressed attitudes) and overt behaviour (buying).

Never let yourself be goaded into taking seriously problems about words and their meanings. What must be taken seriously are questions of fact, and assertions about facts; theories and hypotheses; the problems they solve; and the problems they raise (Popper, 1976).

perfectly in line with the researchers' prior beliefs. The idea that consumers have 'relationships' with brands is an old idea, which is routinely repackaged by marketing consultants. Kevin Roberts' Lovemarks website (www.lovemarks.com) is a classic, and quite humorous, example. To quote, 'Lovemarks are brands that create an intimate emotional connection that you simply can't do without. Ever' (Roberts, 2004).[10]

A more down-to-earth view is that if buyers don't care deeply about a brand then they could be easily lured away to buy another brand. Yet even this supposedly common-sense statement is actually an untested empirical assumption. It's just as plausible to argue that a lack of caring is the cornerstone of ongoing loyalty.

Connection to a brand

Consumers are busy people. They have hundreds of thousands of brands vying for their attention. Thanks to the competitive modern economy, and government regulation, most of these options are sound. Therefore, the choice of brand is trivial compared to the decision of whether or not to purchase from the category. And aside from cars, houses and a minority of other categories, even the decision to buy from the category is a minor one, 'Shall I have a snack or wait until lunch?'

Brands are a necessary evil: they add a layer of complexity to the buying decision, but they also allow for routines ('Ah, there's my brand' or, 'Oh yes, I've heard of that one'); such habits make buying easier—automatic even. From cars to canned soup, routine results in passionless[11] brand loyalty. Also, we're usually so unaware of our habits that we barely notice

---

10 Saatchi and Saatchi's Kevin Roberts says he came up with his 'Lovemarks' idea late one evening after a couple of bottles of red wine. He claims to have done research to 'prove' the idea!

11 This is not to say that emotions play an unimportant role in decision-making and viewing of advertising. The vital role of emotion in decision-making and processing of information is now well established. But it is a huge unrealistic leap to say that this means consumers are, or must be, passionately attached to brands. Most emotions are not particularly heated—indeed neuroscientists say that most emotional responses are so slight that we fail to even feel them. Love is a many-splendoured thing, but not a big part of brand buying.

that we eat the same meals, shop from the same shops, etc. And, as we've seen, loyalty is rarely exclusive; it's nothing like loyalty to a sports team or a country. Buyers typically have a number of brands that they routinely buy, so 100% exclusive loyalty is much rarer than marketers expect.

Marketing texts sometimes dismiss these buying patterns as simply a case of the messy real world deflecting customers from their true intentions. But this interpretation doesn't fit the facts when attitudes, perceptions and intentions are measured. Consumers' thoughts and plans also show this prosaic uncommitted loyalty.

Brand knowledge, attitudes and intentions

Long ago marketing wisdom was that Avis buyers rented from Avis and Hertz buyers rented from Hertz. So if Hertz had 23% market share in a particular country, it was assumed that 23% of car renters used Hertz. As soon as marketing scientists starting looking at ongoing panel records of real-world repeat buying they realised the error of their assumption. Buyers are polygamous; brands share consumers. In the long term, 23% market share means that most category consumers use Hertz, but on average, they only use Hertz not much more than 23% of the time.

The story is similar with attitudes, perceptions and intentions (i.e. people's thoughts about brands). If surveys show that 30% of people say Hertz rents attractive, clean cars then the common assumption is that 30% of people believe this and 70% don't. While the reality is that a lot of people believe this (or remember they believe this), but just not all of the time.

Let me explain. We can see the fickle (actually probabilistic) nature of people's beliefs if we ask them the same question more than once. This is seldom done in market and social research. Surveys generally ask different people each time, which is why even experienced market researchers are generally unaware of this phenomenon.[12] If, on the first survey, 30% of

---

12 This law-like pattern has now been reported and replicated many times in the academic scientific literature, covering many product categories and different question types in the US, Europe, Asia and Australia; for example, Castleberry et al., 1994; Dall'Olmo Riley et al., 1997; Dolnicar & Rossiter, 2008; Rungie et al., 2005; Sharp et al., 2002; Sharp & Winchester, 2002.

people agreed with the statement, 'Hertz rents attractive cars', then on any subsequent survey the figure is also usually very close to 30%. This (misleadingly) suggests a great stability of beliefs. But, if we analyse the answers of each individual we see something startling. Typically, only about half the people who on the first survey agreed with the statement do so again on the second survey, and an equal number of people who did not agree with the statement the first time now agree with it. So the overall level of agreement remains at 30% but the repeat or stability rate (people saying yes both times) is only half (i.e. 50%). Scale-type questions show the same instability.

Table 7.3: Image belief stability survey to survey, Australian financial services brands

Survey: agreement with the statement, 'Would value me as a whole person not just a transaction'.

Brands	Initial agreement (%)	Repeated agreement (%)	Respondents who agreed in both surveys (%)
ANZ	11	53	.53 x 11 = 6%
St George	11	35	.35 x 11 = 4%
NAB	11	44	.44 x 11 = 5%
Colonial	6	33	.33 x 6 = 2%
Average repeat rate		37	

Source: Ehrenberg-Bass Institute.

Note: Repeat rates are always low; usually under 50% of those who agreed with the statement on one survey do so on another interview.

Only half (or less) of the respondents who agreed with the statement ('Would value me as a whole person not just a transaction') agreed again when interviewed again. However, this does not mean that people are becoming increasingly cynical about how banks value them. Overall, the brands get similar scores survey to survey, because every person who no longer votes for the brand is matched by someone who now votes for it (i.e. some of the people who did not agree with this statement on the first interview do so on the second). This instability in response does not mean that those who agreed on the first interview but not the second have fundamentally changed their minds about the brand. It's just that they sometimes think this, so on some interviews you catch them saying it, and some you don't.

This phenomenon applies to all brands, and to all image beliefs, attitudes, purchase intentions and awareness measures. Table 7.4 gives examples across different attitudinal or image statements and across different categories. We can see that the repeat rate varies from brand to brand; it also varies across different beliefs. That's because the repeat rate largely depends on the overall response (agreement) level for that belief and brand. Logically, if on each survey 100% of respondents agreed with a statement (e.g. *How Brands Grow* is a superb book) then the repeat rate must also be 100%—each survey can only record a score of 100% if everyone agrees. However, for beliefs that score less than 100% their repeat rate could be 100% or it could be lower (i.e. a score of 30% in each survey could be because 30% of people agree on every interview, or everyone agrees but only 30% of the time, or something in between). In the real world we find the repeat agreement level is usually far lower than 100%, and we can predict this based on the level of initial agreement—this is

Table 7.4: Image belief stability survey to survey, multiple categories, different types of image belief

Category	Brand image belief	Initial agreement (%)	Repeated agreement (%)
Fast food outlets	Good for a snack	29	56
Banks	Progressive	22	47
Banks	Expert in the areas it deals in	21	48
Insurance	Provides fast service	17	42
Supermarkets	Sells low-quality fruit	14	36
Liquor/spirits	Unique	10	36

Note: Repeat rates are typically low. Usually under 50% of those people who agreed with the statement on one survey do so on another interview.

the whole story, the repeat rate has little to do with the type of belief or other factors.[13]

This doesn't mean that our attitudes and beliefs are random, but rather that our individual brand memories, like our brand buying, are probabilistic. We each have a steady, ongoing propensity to think something, and for most of our beliefs that propensity is not 100%. Not surprisingly, whether or not we recall a belief is highly dependent on the situation,[14] and is very much affected by the cues that are used to elicit the belief, and can change depending on what other things were going through our head at the time.

Our brand-buying behaviour is like this: I might choose Avis 60% of the time, but that doesn't mean that sometimes I won't choose Hertz (indeed it suggests that I definitely will sometimes choose Hertz) even two or three times in a row. This behaviour appears to be random, even though it isn't; each time I buy Avis or Hertz there are particular reasons for this. But those reasons are so variable that anyone watching my choices from a distance might think I was merely tossing a coin to make my choice (a coin that just happened to be weighted 60% in favour of Avis).

So perhaps our attitudes merely reflect our buying. Our behaviour has a strong affect on our attitudes. But also, the fickle nature of our intentions (or their recall) is one of the many causes of our probabilistic buying patterns. Presumably attitudes play a role, albeit a small one, in the weighting of that mental coin.

The key discovery is that most of what we think about brands is *not absolute.* It is natural to tick the survey box that says we are completely satisfied with the brand and one hour later tick the 'only somewhat satisfied'

---

13 Anne Sharp (2002) showed that the repeat rate is a bit higher than expected if university students are the respondents (i.e. probably due to experiment artificiality). Dolnicar and Rossiter (2008) were unpleasantly surprised by the discovery of these low repeat rates and sought to dismiss the phenomenon as a methodological artefact. They attempted a variety of methodology variations on surveys of university student respondents and reported a minuscule increase in stability of response above expected.

14 Amazingly many consumer behaviour textbooks still today, in spite of decades of counter evidence, say that attitudes (positive or negative evaluations about something) are enduring and situation a-specific. If we define attitudes like this then we hold very few attitudes indeed!

box. Indeed, most of what we think about brands is so trivial, so barely thought through, that we will happily change our mind in a second.[15] Actually, it's misleading for me to talk about changing of minds. It's more apt to say that we haven't completely made up our minds yet. Or rather that we have made up our minds to *sometimes* think/like/buy the brand.

Therefore, attitudinal commitment to brands (or to buying them) is much weaker than marketing mythology makes out. But it can exist; for example, the Apple computer on which this book is being typed is rather dear to me personally. Which leads us to question whether it is possible for a brand to build exceptional emotional or symbolic based loyalty. How important to a brand are these special, committed customers? Have some brands excelled at building passionate user bases?

Brand fanatics

It's long been fashionable in marketing to uphold brand fanatics as ideal customers. While most buyers who are 100% loyal to a brand are simply light category buyers, there are a few customers who regularly buy from the category and yet are very loyal to one brand. There are also a few buyers who are passionate about a brand. How important are these people? Who are they? How does a brand attract more passionate consumers?

Don Gorske is a perfect example. This Wisconsin resident has consumed more than 23 000 Big Macs; he claims that the Big Mac constitutes more than 90% of his solid food intake. We know that he's eaten more than 23 000 Big Macs because he records the ongoing total in a notebook. This apparently is just one example of his obsessive behaviour. Don Gorske, to put it mildly, is a little odd.[16] Every brand has a few very loyal and heavy buyers, a few passionate advocates.

---

15   My young daughter has many favourites, many most favourite toys, many most favourite sweets, a number of best friends. We adults know not to make such illogical statements, or at least we try. However, I expect that my daughter's innocent language is more truthful.

16   According to Morgan Spurlock, director of the movie *Super Size Me*, Don Gorske stores the boxes from all the Big Macs he has eaten in his attic. Wikipedia also reports that Don proposed to his wife in his favourite McDonald's car park. See <http://en.wikipedia.org/wiki/Don_Gorske>.

The Lovemarks website lists thousands of brands that have been nominated as Lovemarks by visitors to the website. These are brands that some people feel passionate about (or at least feel so some of the time). The Lovemarks list is moderated and nominees have to make a case for a brand's inclusion. Yet the list still includes prosaic brands such as 7-Eleven. Also, Air New Zealand, Continental Airlines, Delta Airlines, Air Jamaica, KLM, Korean Air, Qantas and Swiss Air all got nominated, as did many other airlines. Among car manufacturers, General Motors, Ford, Honda, Mazda, Mitsubishi, Mercedes, Nissan, Toyota and Saturn have all been nominated.[17] This shows that any brand can have a few fans, a few Don Gorskes; but, it does not show that some brands are special or that these fans are of any financial or strategic consequence to marketers. These make for an entertaining story and that's all. Advertising agencies, who in general know very little about buyer behaviour, love these stories.

Brand loyalty: Harley Davidson and Apple

Most people merely buy a computer. Apple Macintosh customers fall in love (*New York Times*, 2 April 1998).

There is no product on the planet that enjoys the devotion of a Macintosh computer. Famously dedicated to their machines, many Mac fans eat, sleep and breathe Macintosh (*The Cult of the Mac* by Leander Kahney, 2004).

Baba Shiv, a professor of marketing at the Stanford Graduate School of Business, compares Apple's fan base to Harley-Davidson motorcycle riders who pass over arguably higher-quality Japanese bikes ('Apple fans loyal despite iPod, iphone 3G woes', CNN, 2008).[18]

Brands like Harley Davidson and Apple are the poster children for emotion-based brand loyalty. They are regularly cited as having passionate,

---

17   If the Ford car that you'd just chosen and paid for had been stolen, but a kind millionaire, hearing your story, sent you a new similar model Chrysler—would you mind in any way? A few (ungrateful) people might wish a little that they'd been sent a Ford (there are all types in this world), but I suspect not many.

18   <http://edition.cnn.com/2008/TECH/biztech/08/29/apple.loyal.ap/index.html>.

highly loyal customer bases—though few writers provide evidence to back up such claims. Also, no one questions why this loyalty failed to protect Harley Davidson from losing market share to Japanese brands, or Apple to PC clones.

I'm sure it is true that tattoo engravers (if this is the right word) receive more requests for Harley Davidson tattoos than they do for Kelloggs Cornflakes tattoos (this slightly ludicrous example provided by Parker and Stuart, 1997) but this says more about the respective product categories than it does about brand purchasing behaviour.[19]

What are the buying facts about Apple and Harley Davidson loyalty? First, just like other brands, their customers are polygamously loyal to a number of brands. The Harley Davidson's share of category requirements (SCR) metric is reported at about 33%. In other words, Harley Davidson buyers purchase other bikes twice as often as they buy Harleys. This is a very normal sort of loyalty figure for a brand. Similarly, Apple's repeat-buying level is much lower than 100% and is not very different from its competitors; for example, see Table 7.5.

Table 7.5: Apple owners show only moderately higher loyalty

Brand	Repeat (%)
Dell	71
Apple	55
HP/Compaq	52
Gateway	52

Source: MetaFacts Inc., 2002–03 <www.technologyuserprofile.com>.

19　And the fact that Harley Davidson riders are more likely to have tattoos of any sort than the average breakfast cereal buyer (i.e. a statistical selection effect). And that first purchases of motorbikes and tattoos tend to coincide, whereas consumers tend to be first introduced to Cornflakes at an age when their mum won't allow them to get a tattoo, even if they wanted one.

Given what we know about the double jeopardy law (see Chapter 2), Apple's repeat-buying level is slightly high; that is, more Apple owners make their next purchase an Apple computer than we would expect, given Apple's market share. A realistic explanation for this loyalty is that Apple owners would have to swap operating systems, and perhaps replace software, if they switch away from Apple. In comparison, a Gateway owner can switch to HP or Dell (or many dozens of other brands) and use the same operating system and software. This factor alone sufficiently explains Apple's slight loyalty advantage, leaving little room for the effect of passionate commitment. This is not to say that Harley Davidson and Apple don't have brand fanatics, but these customers are a small group, and their numbers are not much larger than the number of passionate fans of competitor brands.

A segmentation analysis of US Harley Davidson riders (Swinyard, 1995) shows that the largest segment (40% of owners) receive little psychological satisfaction from riding. More than the other owners of Harleys, people in this segment agree with statements such as:

- most of the time my motorcycle is just parked
- I like wearing a helmet when riding
- I don't know many other people that ride motorcycles.

These Harley riders are also least likely to agree that, 'My bike is everything to me.' Yet this group represents almost 50% of Harley Davidson's sales revenue.

At the other end of the spectrum, stereotypically fanatical Harley bikers earn the least but spend the most money each year on accessories for their bike. They are also the Harley owners most likely to like tattoos and drink beer; they are also the owners who are the least likely to read a book. These people represent less than 10% of Harley owners and they are the least likely to have bought their bike new, so they represent a mere 3.5% of Harley Davidson's sales revenue.

The 'Hog Heaven' segment is the other owner group that might be classified as passionate brand loyalists; they disagree with statements like,

'I like bikes with plastic farings and engine covers', and are most likely to agree with, 'When I'm on my bike people seem to be admiring me'. While many Harley owners in this segment are well paid, they spend the least on accessories for their bike and buy the smallest models. Consequently, they represent less than 10% of Harley Davidson's sales revenue.

Overall, the owners who rate highest on Harley zeal[20] are worth the least to the company per customer. Additionally, they contribute little revenue because these passionately loyal segments are very small.

Customer advocacy

Even if these brand fanatics fail to turn their passion into sales revenue, it might be nice to think that they act as unpaid ambassadors for the company, broadcasting positive word of mouth. Certainly some brand fanatics do. But remember there aren't many of these people, and their capacity to spread positive brand messages by word of mouth is limited (for example, by the number of people they know).

Capacity to spread positive brand messages by word of mouth is also limited by the degree of new information that is available. This is why research shows that new customers tend to tell more people about the brand than people who have been buying it for a long while (East & Hammond, 2005); for established customers, the brand is no longer news. So loyalty and propensity to give word of mouth are not strongly linked.

Conclusion

We try to bring our attitudes in line with our behaviour. Since brands aren't very important to us, brand buying tends to have a strong effect on our rather weak attitudes—we like what we buy. Our attitudes reflect the divided nature of our brand loyalty. Attitudes also have a weak reinforcing

---

20   Harley Zeal refers to the degree that respondents agreed with statements like, 'I think Harleys are the best bikes in the world', and disagreed with statements like, 'I like good bikes wherever they are made', 'I like the spacecraft look of bikes today', and 'All things considered, I think Japanese bikes are the best' (see Swinyard, 1995).

effect on our current behaviour, so we feel comfortable with our repertoires. Within every brand's customer base there are a few people who feel much more attitudinally committed to the brand. It may be part of their self-image, used to signal what sort of person they are to themselves and to others. But the marketing consequences of these brand fan(atic)s turn out to be very limited. Most of a brand's customers think and care little about the brand, but the brand manager should care about these people because they represent most of the brand's sales; the brand needs these people if it is to increase its sales.

These consumer insights help explain the discoveries and recommendations concerning buying behaviour and brand growth in Chapters 2, 3 and 4.

8

Differentiation versus Distinctiveness

Byron Sharp & Jenni Romaniuk

Rather than striving for meaningful, perceived differentiation, marketers should seek meaningless distinctiveness. Branding lasts, differentiation doesn't.

THOU SHALT DIFFERENTIATE

Textbooks emphatically tell marketers that differentiation must be the centrepiece of their marketing strategy:

- 'if marketing is seminally about anything it is about ... differentiating ... All else is derivative of that and only that' (Theodore Levitt)
- 'each advertisement must make a proposition ... not just puffery [it must say] buy this product and you will get this specific benefit ... one that the competition does not offer' (Rosser Reeves)
- 'differentiation is the cornerstone of successful marketing' (Philip Kotler)
- 'the differentiation must be meaningful to customers ... if a brand fails to differentiate then consumers have no basis for choosing it over others. Without differentiation a loyal customer base cannot be created or sustained' (David Aaker).

Practically every university marketing textbook is called something like *Marketing Management* or *Marketing Principles*, while almost every consumer behaviour textbook has the title *Consumer Behaviour*. The chapter headings in these books are also strikingly similar. These books hardly ever disagree with one another. Ironically, they are a very poor example of the differentiation they preach—textbook authors don't seem to take their own advice.

In spite of nearly every textbook telling marketers to strive for differentiation, real-world competition is largely about competitive matching rather than avoiding competitors by delivering differences. Furthermore, textbooks offer no evidence, beyond selective case studies, that differentiation leads to brand growth or profitability. This doesn't mean that there aren't meaningfully differentiated brands that are growing and profitable, but the empirical fact is that most category leaders have a great many very similar rivals.

Every category has some brands (or variants) that are more expensive and higher quality. Sometimes there are brands that are vastly more expensive—but these up-market brands face many similarly high-priced competitors within their sub-category. Some brands are a bit faster, a tad sweeter, a touch more stylish, slightly trendier or provide a marginally better service. Yet, there is not much difference between them, and it's surprising how many similar brands a market will support. This leads to some interesting questions:

1 Can advertising imbue brands with special values? (In other words, can marketing differentiate functionally similar brands?)
2 Do buyers need to perceive a meaningful difference to regularly buy a brand (i.e. to show a preference or loyalty)?[1]

The answers to these questions strike at the heart of much modern marketing thinking and practice. The answers interest both practising

---

1   The answers to these two questions are: 1) Largely no, this isn't the main effect of advertising; 2) No.

marketers and their civic-minded critics. It's time empirical science was applied to these questions.

Special values

One explanation for the plethora of rival brands that exist is that advertising has imbued each brand with a different perceived meaning that consumers value.

Marketers routinely measure brand perceptions. Sometimes for very practical reasons, for example, they want to find out how many people know their store is open on Saturday, or whether women perceive them differently to men. However, today it's common for marketers to measure more esoteric perceptions, like whether consumers imbue the brand with human personality traits. A significant amount of brand management time is spent developing huge batteries of highly subjective perceptual cues to measure.[2]

The data that such image (brand health/equity) surveys generate are often subjected to multivariate statistical techniques, or the even more obscure proprietary analyses that many market research agencies peddle. These are typically designed to highlight differences between brands, but usually fail to convey how big these differences really are—or how they relate to actual buying behaviour. By now this might strike you as odd (and not good practice), given that we saw previously (in Chapter 5) that buyers of one brand perceive that brand in much the same way as buyers of rival brands perceive their brand—the 'I love my Mum' pattern.

Bigger brands have many more customers (see Chapter 2), and so they have more people who are likely to respond to an image survey question. Consequently, larger brands tend to score higher on any image question, because they will have more customers among the survey respondents.

---

2   These perceptual cues are developed with little prior thought about how these cues should be interpreted in relation to one another; for example, what does it mean if a brand scores well on being 'a good business partner' but scores poorly on 'understands our needs'? Consequently, a great degree of effort goes into untestable post-hoc explanations of what a subtle shift in brand image might mean.

Their buyers are also slightly more loyal (i.e. they buy more frequently), which enhances their propensity to think/say things about the brand. So, even in survey data that only reports on the perceptions of each brand's buyers, brands with larger market share will score higher.

To understand if a brand really is perceived differently by the market you have to remove this usage (i.e. more buyers) effect. What is not well known—or is rarely discussed by market researchers—is that once the usage effect is removed there is little sign of brands having unique images. For example, Table 8.1 lists the percentage of respondents (who are familiar with a brand) who associate a brand (e.g. FedEx) with a particular image attribute (e.g. trusted). This data was published in a market research journal (Whitlark & Smith, 2001) to show how complicated image data are supposed to be. However, Professor Martin Collins (2002) subsequently showed that if you are familiar with the law-like patterns you can 'see the wood for the trees' without complicating things with multivariate statistics. In Table 8.1, brands are simply ranked in order of the number of respondents who were familiar with them.

The data in Table 8.1 is ranked using familiarity as a proxy for usage; it's only a rough proxy, yet the ranking still produces the sort of patterns seen when only users of each brand have their perceptions measured. These main patterns are:

1 Some attributes always score higher than others (e.g. more than 90% for 'trusted' compared with only 30% for 'essential').[3]

2 All brands gain very similar scores—with a slight double jeopardy sub-pattern (i.e. smaller brands score slightly lower).

Therefore, all brands are seen in much the same way by those familiar with them. Even small brands get a similar endorsement from their few buyers.

---

3   Generally image scores reflect the law of proto-typicality, in that attributes that describe the product category well (e.g. 'lends money' for banking) score higher than less prototypical attributes (Romaniuk & Sharp, 2000). Here the attributes are abstract, so this pattern is more difficult to discern. Abstract attributes like 'trust' have been shown to reflect past usage (e.g. see Romaniuk & Bogomolova, 2005).

Table 8.1: Association of brands with attributes

Company	Trusted	Efficient	Rapport	Relevant	Solution	Innovative	Essential	Average
					Attributes (%)			
FedEx	95	94	84	79	69	60	39	**74**
A	96	95	85	81	72	63	37	**76**
Nokia	96	83	75	67	65	**89**	22	**71**
B	97	87	82	76	75	47	32	**71**
C	94	78	72	70	75	54	46	**70**
Oracle	93	83	73	53	60	**85**	19	**67**
D	94	90	85	58	81	66	23	**71**
Average	**94**	**87**	**79**	**69**	**71**	**66**	**31**	**71**

Source: Collins, 2002.

Once these patterns are known, it is easy to spot the few exceptions; for example, Nokia and Oracle (two technology brands) are considered more 'innovative'. This is not an unexpected or exciting story.

This is not to say that some brands aren't perceived differently to their rival brands, but any sizable differences in perception usually reflect very obvious functional aspects; for example, American brands are perceived as American, French as French and expensive brands as expensive. Perceptual surveys are still useful—they are just far less deterministic and mysterious than they are typically portrayed. Their utility lies in marketers using them to ensure that all their advertising is truly branded (i.e. to look like you, you need to know how the market already sees you).

Brand personality

It's very difficult to find exotic image attributes (i.e. not related to obvious functional features) that substantially differentiate rival brands. Brand personality is a recent attempt. Long ago, marketing researchers began investigating the impact of a buyer's personality on their brand choice. This was quickly shown to be inconsequential. The famous study into Ford versus Chevrolet buyers by Franklin B Evans was one of the first to challenge this notion: the study found no difference in the personality traits of the different brand buyers (Evans, 1959).

However, personality researchers persisted. The goal became to identify the human personality a brand is reflecting. Interest in brand personality heightened with the publication of Jennifer Aaker's (1997) 'brand personality' scale, which measures the human characteristics that consumers associate with brands, such as charm or ruggedness.

However, it turns out that personality perceptions are like all other image attributes (i.e. users of different brands see their respective brands in much the same way). But brand personality perceptions score very poorly— it turns out that consumers are reluctant to view brands as people (i.e. only 5% think brand X is rugged).[4] These perceptions, that are weakly held by

---

4   We were relieved to find that very few people (around 3%) in Britain consider their condiment brands to be 'charming'.

the population, are also weakly held by individuals (of the 5% who think the brand is rugged in one interview, only about a quarter of these people (about 1%) will repeat the assertion when re-interviewed). Yet a number of marketers adopted the brand personality concept without asking for such empirical evidence first—like medieval doctors (see Chapter 1).

Unique associations

If brands were really differentiated in the minds of consumers, we might expect successful brands to have unique image attributes (i.e. consumers associate an image with only one brand). It's long been argued that brand equity rests on strong and unique associations. But a thorough examination of the image data of 130 brands in 13 product and service categories shows that people rarely (about 3% of the time) see a single brand as being exclusively associated with a particular image (Gaillard & Romaniuk, 2007). More successful brands do not have proportionally more unique associations, nor do customers with greater preference for a brand hold more unique associations than those with less preference. Instead, the level of brand uniqueness—as designated by the proportion of associations customers hold for one brand only—has been shown to be simply negatively correlated with the number of brands in the category: a brand is more likely to be perceived as the only brand with a particular quality if it has few competitors.

Meaningful differentiation

Differentiation is deemed to be an essential part of marketing strategy. It is taught more like religion than hard-nosed business: differentiated brands will inherit all the customers and profits; it's all or nothing and we are told we must 'differentiate or die' (Trout & Rivkin, 2000).

Marketing texts use a motivational perspective—they talk of a meaning-ful, perceived difference that provides buyers with their reason to purchase and be loyal to a brand (Aaker, 2001; Kotler, 1994). Undifferentiated new entrants to a market are supposed to be likely to fail because no customer is motivated to buy them (Davidson, 1976). It is believed that established brands need to maintain their point of difference in order to stay desirable to their customers. Breakthroughs in perceived differentiation—achieved either through product features (e.g. Apple's original, candy-coloured iMac) or image-building advertising (e.g. Marlboro man)—are seen as pathways to growth.

The marketing literature explicitly states that a brand's differentiation has to be perceived by customers and must be valued. This valued difference doesn't have to be a product feature, and can be symbolic or emotional. Some marketing texts even suggest that a brand's differentiation can be based on what, in reality, are meaningless product features, such as Folgers 'flaked coffee crystals' (Carpenter, Glazer & Nakamoto, 1994)—so long as it is noticed, believed and valued by consumers. Perception is reality, as many marketing commentators point out.

The advertising principle of promoting a 'unique selling proposition' (USP) (Reeves, 1961) reflects this theory. Advertising that does not give buyers a reason to buy the product is thought to be ineffective. Although, some have challenged this orthodoxy by arguing that advertising can work effectively without a USP or a means of persuasion (see Chapter 9).

Yet, in spite of these strong beliefs, or perhaps because of them, very little is known about brand differentiation. Consider these questions:

- How different are brands perceived to be?
- Do buyers need to perceive a meaningful difference to repeatedly buy a brand?
- Are some brands far more differentiated than their rivals? Does this mean their buyers are more loyal? Are these brands more profitable? Are they growing faster?

In spite of all the marketing books that preach differentiation, they offer scant evidence to answer these questions.

Real world differentiation

There are very good reasons to doubt the picture of differentiation presented in many texts. Much of the empirical evidence that is presented in this book does not sit well with this picture.

Differentiation undoubtedly exists. The idea that brands are identical commodities is fiction; for a start, they have different names that can be used by buyers to develop loyalties and show preference.[5] Equally importantly, there is a tremendous amount of situational differentiation, for example:

- this brand is here now, while the others are not
- I know where this bakery is
- this one has my size
- this is the only one in red
- I'm in the mood for chocolate
- it was the one I noticed
- it was the one that came to mind.

These situational differences affect all brands; this means that they all enjoy some differentiation. But is there also differentiation at the brand level? Do some buyers (across time and buying situations) see and value a difference?

The first thing that should make us question the importance of differentiation is that loyalty does not vary significantly between rival brands (see Chapter 2). Loyalty definitely exists, but it is a characteristic of consumer behaviour, rather than being driven by brand differentiation. This means that all brands should benefit from loyalty. But if there is substantial differentiation at the brand level, then why doesn't loyalty differ much between brands? Why are niche brands, with small but highly loyal customer bases, not commonplace?

The second thing we should consider is that if brand-level differentiation is strong then a brand should appeal more to a particular type of person who particularly values the brand's style of differentiated offer. Yet, as discussed in Chapter 5, brand-user profiles don't differ much—competing brands in a category sell to very similar customer bases (Kennedy & Ehrenberg, 2000; Kennedy & Ehrenberg, 2001a). Brands with vastly different prices (and quality) have different user profiles; expensive brands

---

5   See the results of Tucker's experiment described in Chapter 7.

tend to be bought by wealthier people. But within their competitive set, the brands' user bases are similar: Versace's buyers are similar to Gucci's and Nike's buyers are similar to Adidas's.

Differentiation theory suggests there should be a great deal of market partitioning (where brands share more or fewer customers than they would be expected to according to their respective market shares). Brands that are very differentiated from one another should share very few customers; brands that are positioned in a similar manner should share many customers. Yet the widespread fit of the duplication of purchase law, which states brands share customers with other brands in line with their relative shares, shows that partitioning is generally slight (see Chapter 6).

If brands vary in their degree of differentiation, we might expect to see them exhibit different price elasticities, as customers of more differentiated brands would be less sensitive to price. However, price elasticities seem to vary more with the context of the price change (see Chapter 10). This again suggests that brands within a category have similar levels of differentiation.

Finally, we must consider the strong, empirically grounded mathematical model, the NBD-Dirichlet (Goodhardt, Ehrenberg & Chatfield, 1984). This model effectively assumes that brands compete as undifferentiated choice options of varying popularity. The real world conforms to this model, with the NBD-Dirichlet successfully predicting a wide variety of brand performance metrics in dozens of product categories, different countries and across time (Ehrenberg, Uncles & Goodhardt, 2004).[6]

---

6 The Dirichlet even correctly predicts the slight asymmetry in competition between large and small brands observed in empirical work on price changes (Kamakura & Russell, 1989; Scriven & Ehrenberg, 2004); in doing so it explains this phenomenon as simply a statistical selection effect, not due to differences in perceived differentiation. A small brand is more affected by actions of a large brand than a large brand is affected by actions of a small brand. For example, it is likely that wherever the small brand is stocked so is the big brand, but not vice-versa. So if the big brand runs a promotion it will affect the small brand in all the locations that the small brand is sold, whereas the small brand's promotions will affect the big brand only in those places where it shares distribution with the small brand.

Every category has brands that differ in price and quality (referred to as 'vertical differentiation' by economists). Sometimes a category contains brands that are vastly more expensive than the other brands in the category. This price difference shows up in the dissimilarity of the different (i.e. cheaper and more expensive) brand's user bases. The price difference is also exhibited in the more expensive brand's departure from the duplication of purchase law and NBD-Dirichlet benchmarks. The fact that this evidence is not often seen for other brands suggests weak levels of differentiation at best.[7]

This body of theory and empirical evidence does not support the traditional role of differentiation presented in much marketing literature, nor does it support a 'perfect competition' (commodity) model. Differentiation undoubtedly exists, but empirically grounded theory suggests differentiation is best thought of as a category level (rather than brand level) phenomenon. In summary, differentiation theory is like the neo-classical, economic, perfect competition model, in that it describes an abstract ideal world and not the one that real brands compete within.

Icon brands

It's not just the buying of everyday, run-of-the-mill brands that causes the patterns reported above. These laws also apply to 'icon brands', which are brands that are supposed to represent the height of marketing excellence and consumer bonding. For example, Nike is considered (by the CEO of Saatchi and Saatchi, Kevin Roberts (2004, pp. 78–9)) to be a Lovemark brand, which is a brand that inspires 'loyalty beyond reason'. Yet an analysis by Dr John Dawes clearly shows that Nike conforms to the double jeopardy law and the duplication of purchase law: Nike's buyers are not 100% loyal; they give it no more loyalty than it should receive given its market share (i.e. Nike's loyalty is less than Adidas' in some markets). Nike sells to the same sort of people as other sports brands,

---

7   It must be noted that within these expensive/luxury sub-categories the rival brands compete as if there is little differentiation.

to similar demographics, social classes and psycho-geo-demo-graphics. These patterns in real buying behaviour raise serious questions about the degree to which buyers perceive rival brands to be different.

Perceived differentiation

So how do buyers choose between branded options? Do buyers need to perceive that the brand they are purchasing is different? Do they need another reason to buy the brand (other than offering the benefits of the category, e.g. it tastes like ice-cream or it works like a credit card)? Systematic study across product and service categories, countries, survey methods and questions types reveals two robust patterns:

1 Buyers of a brand perceive very weak differentiation—yet this does not stop them loyally buying a particular brand.
2 A brand's level of perceived differentiation is very similar to their rivals.

Table 8.2 reports the proportion of a selection of brand's regular buyers who agree that the brand is different or unique.

Table 8.2: Brand user perceptions of differentiation in the soft drink (UK) and banking (Australia) categories

Brand	Different (%)	Unique ($)	Either (%)	Brand	Different (%)	Unique (%)	Either (%)
Coca-Cola	8	13	19	ANZ	12	4	15
Diet Coke	9	8	15	CBA	12	12	19
Pepsi-Cola	7	10	15	NAB	8	12	12
Fanta	8	5	12	Westpac	9	6	11
Pepsi Max	9	10	19	St George	26	16	32
Schweppes	6	9	13				
Canada Dry	10	9	17				
Average	**9**	**9**	**16**	**Average**	**13**	**10**	**18**

Note: Differentiation scores are typically low.

Source: Ehrenberg-Bass Institute.

All the markets we have examined, whether using our own or others' data, follow a similar pattern: an average of 10% of any brands' users think their brand is different. It could be that these responses reflect apathy when responding to research questionnaires; however, there are three indicators that this is not the case. First, within the markets there were exceptional brands that had obvious functional differences. For example, Aldi supermarkets, which do not stock national brands, scored 67% for 'different'; while in the fast food category, sandwich-only brand Subway achieved 50% for 'unique' when put in a competitive set with McDonald's, Domino's and KFC. So respondents could indicate when something was perceived as differentiated. However, most brands were seldom perceived as such. Second, differences in categories were reflected in the responses. Third, the results show expected differences between markets; for example, soft drinks are more differentiated than water. Spirits and skincare—two categories we deliberately chose because they are highly 'image driven' and supported by vast amounts of brand advertising expenditure—both showed among the highest levels of perceived differentiation (although still low).

To check whether this finding was simply an artefact of the measure, we also tried a forced choice 5-point scale (where 1 is not at all descriptive and 5 is extremely descriptive). The average score was 2.5: few brands scored higher than the neutral midpoint of 3, and none had a mean as high as 4 (a score that would indicate respondents *somewhat agreed* the brand was different). Therefore, our finding that consumers hardly see their brands as differentiated is consistent across both a pick-any or a rating scale measure.[8]

There were some systematic deviations from this general pattern, where brands consistently obtained higher response levels. This was for small, higher-priced brands, and is consistent with the notion that more differentiated brands will be smaller. Or, less popular brands are seen to

---

8   This concurs with research that shows that perceptual surveys employing either rating scales, rankings or pick-any all produce similar findings (Barnard & Ehrenberg, 1990; Driesener & Romaniuk, 2006).

be different. There were also some brand-specific deviations; however, these tended to be linked to large functional differences and less to image differentiation. So the majority of buyers do not explicitly state that they perceive their brand to be differentiated from other brands. Therefore, it is questionable whether perceptions of brand differentiation drive buyer behaviour. Buyers don't need to see differentiation to buy a brand, or to keep on buying it.

Table 8.3: Examples of category level results

	Current users who perceive it is different (%)	Current users who perceive it is unique (%)	Current users who perceive it is either (%)	Customers who perceived at least one brand for either attribute (%)
Spirits	20	27	36	71
Supermarkets	25	21	31	72
Skincare products	17	21	30	66
Ice-cream	14	11	20	43
Fast food	16	13	20	64
Banking	13	10	18	73
Soft drinks	11	9	18	76
Condiments	10	9	17	67
F&V drinks	11	8	16	51
Ready sauces	9	7	14	53
Information technology	9	10	14	44
Soups	8	5	12	35
Yoghurt	8	5	11	43
Cars	9	6	11	66
Water	6	6	10	32
Electronics	4	6	8	47
Average	**11**	**10**	**17**	**54**

Source: Romaniuk, Sharp & Ehrenberg, 2007.

Table 8.4—showing some of the brand-level data from the information technology category in Table 8.3—illustrates this with the example of Apple, a poster child for differentiation and customer loyalty (as discussed in Chapter 7). Apple's level of perceived differentiation is higher than other computer brands, but it is not high. Most (77%) of Apple users did not perceive their brand to be different or unique. This seems surprising, given that Apple computers look different and use a different operating system.[9] However, most computer users have little technical knowledge and few would know what an operating system was. Apple Macintosh is a personal computer (PC), with a graphical user interface, a mouse and keyboard, it runs software (e.g. Microsoft Office), sends email, surfs the web, stores files, prints and so on. It is not unreasonable that its users see it as doing very much the same things as other computers. They certainly buy it to do the same things. Few apparently bought it because they wanted a computer that was different; they bought it to be a good useful computer—just as buyers of any other computer brand.[10]

Many marketing texts instruct marketers to strive to make customers perceive valued differences between brands. Yet even marketers of highly successful brands seem to have failed. This leads to the conclusion that perceived differentiation plays little part in the success of brands. It is certainly not a case of 'differentiate or die'; if it were, most of the brands we buy would be gone.

The literature on consumer behaviour has for decades focused on customer perceptions of brand features as the main reason why one brand is chosen over others. This emphasis is misplaced. If buyers of a brand don't often think their brand is different or unique, then presumably this is not the main reason they buy it. We need to look elsewhere for explanations of why customers buy one brand and not another.

---

9 When this survey took place, Apple computers generally ran MacOS 9 and did not yet have the easy ability to run Windows. Other computer brands generally ran Windows 95. Apple was marketing coloured iMacs while competitors' computers were beige or, very occasionally, black.

10 Apple's legendary loyalty also appears to be an exaggeration; see Chapter 7.

Table 8.4: Computer brand users' perceived differentiation

Users of	Different (%)	Unique (%)	Associating the brand with either (%)
HP	4	8	11
Toshiba	11	5	13
Compaq	10	10	18
IBM	16	13	18
Apple	15	25	23
Dell	5	5	5
Average (all)	**9**	**10**	**14**

Note: Only a quarter of Apple users think the brand is different or unique.

Source: Y&R, BAV (Brand Asset Valuator), 1999.

It seems counterintuitive that buyers do not often notice that the brands they use are somehow different from other brands in the market (given that some of the brands are functionally different). This shows that brand choice is a trivial task, as is the choice of deciding whether to not to buy from the product category. So buyers do not spend a great deal of time comparing brands in a category, and so differentiation (relative to other brands) is not noticed. This realisation is counter to many models of information processing; buyers are thought to weigh up brands on the merits of their relative attributes (e.g. Alpert, 1971; Fishbein & Ajzen, 1975; Green, Goldberg & Montemayor, 1981), which implies that buyers know about the differences between brands. However, what empirical evidence shows is that buyers seem to know something about the brands they use, and very little about the ones they don't. This results in the much lower response levels from non-users (compared to that of users).

The main implication for marketing practice is that it isn't essential for marketers to convince buyers that a product is different before they buy it. This should take a considerable weight off marketers' shoulders, because our data shows that such a task must be near impossible. Instead, marketers should focus on achieving the things that do make customers buy a product.

Brands *are* different from one another, and they are perceived as such, but differentiation plays a small role in how brands compete. Consider three brands that are functionally different: Pizza Hut, McDonald's and KFC. Respectively, they sell pizza, burgers and fried chicken. We should expect that McDonald's primarily competes with other burger providers (Wimpys, Burger King, Hungry Jacks, Carl's Jr, etc.); that Pizza Hut competes with other pizza chains (Dominos, Pizza Pizza, Little Caesars, Papa John's, Pizza Haven); and that KFC competes with other chicken outlets (Harold's Chicken Shack, Bojangles, Oporto, Chesters, Red Rooster etc.).[11] According to textbook logic, McDonald's, KFC and Pizza Hut would not compete against one another (or very indirectly). Of course this is nonsense; they are direct competitors; they compete in one big fast food category. Rather than working to differentiate themselves and splinter this fast food category, they actually try to reduce their differentiation; for example, McDonald's advertises that it offers chicken (burgers), KFC advertises that it offers (chicken) burgers and Pizza Hut advertises that it sells chicken (pizza).

Recently, it has been suggested that awareness and salience play a greater role in buyer behaviour and how brands compete than current differentiation theory would suggest (Ehrenberg, Barnard & Scriven, 1997; Romaniuk, 2004a & b). The Ehrenberg-Bass Institute research on perceived differentiation supports this. All brands are 'differentiated' (they do not compete as perfect substitutes), in the sense that for each buyer there are brands that they know well and other brands they think very little about. For each buyer there are many brands he or she never or

---

11   Interestingly, out of pizza, burgers and chicken, chicken is generally the most popular. Yet McDonald's is the largest company—its sales are more than double Pizza Hut's and KFC's sales combined. In most markets McDonald's also has a very substantial mental and physical availability advantage over these two rivals (see Chapter 12).

seldom considers purchasing. But this is not brand differentiation in the sense that buyers perceive some brands as being meaningfully different from others.

Distinctiveness: an alternative perspective

Paradoxically, the reduced emphasis on meaningful differentiation makes branding even more important. Loyalty is underpinned by salience not love/hate. To encourage brand loyalty a brand must stand out so that buyers can easily, and without confusion, identify it. The focus on meaningful, perceived differentiation in marketing literature has distracted from this traditional aspect of branding practice.

The fundamental purpose of branding is to identify the source of the product or service. This is the reason that branding was first developed. Branding must have qualities that distinguish the brand from other competitors. One obvious characteristic is the brand name itself, which is, by law, unique. There are also other distinctive elements that, as part of a brand's identity, can supplement or substitute for the brand name. These qualities help the consumer to notice, recognise and recall the brand—when the brand is advertising and in buying situations. These elements can include:

- colours—such as the Coca-Cola and Vodaphone red
- logos—such as McDonald's golden arches
- taglines—such as Nike's 'Just do it'
- symbols/characters—such as Mickey Mouse's ears
- celebrities—such as Tiger Woods for Nike
- advertising styles—such as MasterCard's 'priceless' campaign.

A distinctive element is anything that shows people what brand a product is. These can be used on packaging and in advertising, in-store displays and sponsorships—they can be used in any marketing activity where the marketer wants the consumer to be able to identify the brand. This might be to build, refresh or reinforce consumer memory structures or to facilitate purchasing by making the brand easier to locate.

The stronger and fresher the links between these distinctive elements and the brand name, the easier it is for the consumer to identify the brand.

Benefits of a distinctive brand

Distinctive brand assets benefit both the marketer and the consumer. A brand loses custom if its potential customers can't find it. Further, communications are more effective if correctly branded. Much has been written about the cluttered environment, the overload of information due to the greater number of choices available. Distinctiveness reduces the need to think, scour and search—thus making life easier for consumers, without them even realising it. This is a very different consumer benefit from that offered by differentiation, and it has an intrinsic value to the consumer. For example, I value service; therefore I seek a brand that will give fabulous service. Consumers do not use American Express because they value the colour blue; but seeing the distinctive blue allows people to easily identify that this ad, piece of direct mail, sponsorship is by Amex (Gaillard, Romaniuk & Sharp, 2005).

Distinctive assets also represent a considerable competitive advantage to brands. Unlike 'meaningful' differentiation, these qualities can be trade-marked and legally protected (Johnson, 1997). It also becomes foolish for a competitor to use the same elements in their advertising, as the advertising is then misattributed to the original brand.

The difference between differentiation and distinctiveness is not just semantics; it is a very real difference that is respected in law.

What makes a distinctive asset?

When determining the strength of the distinctive assets of a brand there are two criteria that are important to consider. These are:

1 uniqueness
2 prevalence.

This assessment must come from consumer research. Marketers and agencies tend not to research and, therefore, they massively over-estimate the strength of their distinctive assets. In turn, this leads to both over-estimating the degree of branding that really exists in advertising copy and over-estimating how easy a brand is to notice on shelf.

The purpose of building strong, distinctive assets is to increase the number of stimuli that can act as identification triggers for a brand. Distinctive assets improve advertising effectiveness by making it more likely for viewers to identify which brand the advertising belongs to. In a shopping environment, distinctive assets make it easier for consumers to notice and purchase a brand.

It is important that each distinctive element is uniquely linked to its brand. If consumers also think of competitors when prompted with that element, then the element fails to act as a brand name substitute. If a shared, distinctive element is substituted for the brand name, the risk is that consumers will think of a competitor rather than the target brand. The second criterion for considering an element to be a distinctive asset is that it is prevalent. This means that the majority of consumers link the brand to the element. A distinctive element that is unique, but unknown, cannot act as a substitute for the brand name because most people who encounter it will not think of the brand name.

Building distinctive assets

Distinctive assets are not inherent; they need to be learned by consumers. Until the links between distinctive elements and the brand are learned they can not function as a substitute for the brand. To successfully teach the link requires a commitment over many years, even decades. For example, the Nike 'swoosh' was first introduced in the 1970s; for a long while it was shown alongside the brand name, prior to being used as a solo brand identifier. The strong recognition that the swoosh has today is because of the consistent investment over many decades.

To build strong, distinctive elements the brand must be consist-ently communicated to consumers across all media and over time. The importance of consistency has been emphasised by many branding com-mentators, and particularly by the proponents of integrated marketing communications. However, this emphasis usually relates to the brand's message and positioning, rather than to the visual, verbal or style of branding elements. Consistency in brand identity is something that many brand strategies lack, particularly across campaigns. For example, when a new campaign is created, most of the attention is placed on what is new and fresh. Just as much attention should be placed on making sure the branding elements are similar and consistent; someone who saw the last marketing campaign should understand that the new campaign comes from the same brand. It is only when there is discipline in this consistency that distinctive brand assets build.

In Chapter 4 we saw how all brands have a 'long tail' of very occasional buyers; because most of a brand's buyers rarely buy and rarely think of it, they are easily confused by inconsistent communication and packaging changes.

A new research focus

While there has been considerable literature on the different elements that could represent distinctive assets, a great deal of this research has been misdirected. It has tried to establish the value of potential distinctive assets to consumers, from a differentiation-style perspective. For example, research into the colours associated with brands often focus on what the colours mean to consumers, or try to identify the best colour for a brand (Bellizzi, Crowley & Hasty, 1983; Grimes & Doole, 1998). However, the real value of building strong links to an element such as a particular colour is not that people may like, say blue more than yellow (and so a brand should choose blue over yellow in its packaging, communications, etc). The value is that if a brand consistently uses blue in its packaging and communications, and it is the only brand that uses blue, consumers will quickly and easily identify that blue represents the brand. This will hopefully mean that colour can replace the brand in some circumstances, or extend the branding quality of any communication beyond simply mentioning or showing the brand name.

Conclusion

Scientific laws, theory and direct empirical evidence challenge the importance placed on meaningful perceived differentiation. Differentiation *does* exist, but the degree of differentiation is weak and varies little between rival brands, and is far less important than it is portrayed. Brands within a category do not vary markedly in their degree of differentiation, perceived or otherwise. While Pizza Hut, McDonald's and KFC sell different products (pizza, burgers and fried chicken, respectively) the reality is that they compete as fast food brands.

This finding has resulted in the presentation of an alternative strategic emphasis: marketing should build distinctive qualities that increase the visibility of the brand in its competitive environment price (i.e. branding matters). Distinctive assets make it easier for consumers to notice, recognise, recall and (importantly) buy the brand. An emphasis on distinctiveness means less trying to find unique selling propositions and more trying to find unique identifying characteristics. Distinctive assets are not what motivate consumers to buy brands; it's how they know where the brand is and what brand they bought. They allow for the development of loyalty.

The next three chapters present empirical evidence on how marketing interventions, like advertising and price promotions, work. Then I return to this topic of how brands compete and what marketers must achieve in order to grow market share over the long term.

How Advertising Really Works

Byron Sharp

Once upon a time there were two little girls, Georgiana and June, who lived in a little French village. Their parents had a beautiful orchard with many lemon trees. So one day they decided to make lemonade. Over time they became very proficient lemonade makers. Each summer, during school vacation, they sold their lemonade to friends and neighbours.

The little girls grew up, got married and moved to the big city. They lived on opposite sides of the town and, sadly, they saw little of each other. However, they both continued to make and market lemonade.

Georgiana had married the owner of a newspaper (her sister June had married a lawyer) and one year she decided to place advertisements for her lemonade in her husband's newspaper. They said 'Georgiana's lemonade: real lemony'. Georgiana's sales steadily grew—eventually she had to source additional supplies of lemons. In the following years, her sales continued to grow, slowly, with occasional jumps when a new store started stocking Georgiana's lemonade.

Meanwhile, the sales of June's lemonade also grew for a while, then for a long time they were steady and then her sales started to slightly decline. One Christmas she discussed this with her sister Georgiana, and on her advice began to advertise. June's advertisements featured the cunningly crafted message 'June's lemonade: lemon goodness'.

Today Georgiana's brand is the largest with slightly more than 60% market share. It is stocked in more stores, it gets more publicity, has more buyers and more people say they prefer it. June's lemonade also continues to sell well and make a profit. She has almost 40% relative market share and her sales decline has stopped. The percentage of June's buyers who say it tastes great is similar to the percentage of buyer's who like the taste of Georgiana's lemonade.

If you accept that Georgiana and June's story is plausible, then you believe advertising works; this is logical, because billions of dollars are spent on advertising. An amazing 2% of the world's GDP is spent on it every year. Yet, things are never as clear as they are in Georgiana and June's world; in the real world, mysteries and contradictions abound. For large brands that have the biggest advertising budgets, sales seldom rise when advertising starts, nor slump when it stops.[1] Also, most buyers say that advertising does not affect them. Even advertising agencies are extremely reluctant to say that advertising causes sales; they'd much rather talk about building brand equity, emotional commitment and added values. In contrast, opponents of advertising say it is a powerful manipulative force. 'Advertising troubles both sociologists and financial directors: the former because they think it works, the latter because they think it does not' (Bullmore, 1999).

What is going on? Who is right? What evidence is there that advertising drives sales? How does advertising really work? How should marketers use advertising? How should marketers measure advertising's effects? This chapter answers these questions and presents a model of brand advertising

---

1   The lack of apparent sales responsiveness to advertising has been observed by the most astute marketers for decades. It is also well documented in academic research on changes in advertising weight (e.g. Hu et al., 2009; Lodish et al., 1995) and advertising elasticities (e.g. Tellis, 2009). The implication that advertising has almost no sales effect is a common misconception arising from this research.

that is consistent with what we know about brand buying behaviour and memory. The shift in thinking is summarised in Table 9.1.

Table 9.1: Advertising

Past world view	Rational or emotional	Message comprehension	Unique selling propositions	Persuasion	Teaching	Positioning
New world view	Emotional and rational	Getting noticed	Relevant associations	Refreshing and building memory structures	Reaching	Salience

Neuroscience and psychology have recently advanced our understanding of how memories and brains work. These discoveries have important implications for advertising, because advertising works by creating and refreshing memories. It is now known that much thinking and decision-making is non-conscious and emotional. Yet traditional theories of advertising are based on a dated view that we are usually rational (occasionally emotional) decision-makers, with near perfect memories.

Before we discuss how advertising works, we first look at the evidence for advertising sales effects (i.e. how advertising nudges buying behaviour). This insight, from marketing science, complements the perspective above. It is a story that has not been told before, yet it provides a deep understanding of how advertising works and why the sales effects are so hard to measure reliably.

The sales response to brand advertising

The purpose of brand advertising is to affect the buying behaviour of consumers. Don't let anyone tell you otherwise. The billions of dollars spent on brand advertising are spent to protect and build sales; logically, this can only happen by affecting buying behaviour and by enhancing and restoring purchase probabilities.

Many people involved in crafting advertising get squeamish with this idea. The reason for this odd behaviour is that they associate sales effects with a limited type of advertising (e.g. 'Sales starts this Thursday' and

'Crazy discounts—buy now, now, now!'). This sort of advertising increases sales, whereas much brand advertising has little or no demonstrable effect on sales figures. This observation leads to the assumption that advertising does something else other than affect buying. So to justify advertising, marketers invoke concepts such as brand equity, commitment and loyalty, often in a very mystical manner. This makes financial directors and hard-nosed CEOs suspect that the money they spend on advertising is going down the drain.

There is solid empirical evidence that brand advertising does produce sales. Yet the effects of advertising are very difficult to see in sales trends. The reasons for this are not well understood. This ignorance means that some people who study sales effects (e.g. econometric modelling consultancies and academics) often get their estimates wrong.

There are two reasons why advertising's sales effects are hard to see in weekly and monthly sales figures (i.e. sales neither jump when advertising starts or increases, nor collapse when it is reduced). The proper effect of advertising on sales is often missed because:

1   The aim of most advertising is to maintain market share. Few companies spend enough (or create good enough advertising) to increase market share or accelerate an upwards trend. Mostly, advertising is used to prevent what (without any advertising) would be a very gentle decline in sales. Much advertising is aimed at preventing competitors' advertising from stealing future sales. This prevention means a brand gets sales, over a long period of time, that it would not have obtained if it had not advertised. So advertising causes sales even if a brand's sales figures are flat.

2   Advertising's sales effects are spread out in time. This means that the effect of today's advertising is layered very thinly across sales figures over a long time period. It typically takes dramatic bursts of expenditure to cause a week's figures to detectably increase.[2]

---

2   Similarly, sales figures don't drop suddenly when advertising is stopped, which is half the reason marketers find it hard to defend their budgets against cuts.

This is particularly the case for large brands, because their advertising expenditure is small in comparison to their other marketing efforts, such as their ongoing word of mouth, their sheer physical presence (shelf space is advertising too) and the already established salience (past advertising effects) in many consumers' heads. Changes in advertising weight are more likely to make weekly sales figures of a small brand move up and down because it doesn't have a large base of sales that are supported by existing market-based assets.

Consequently, statistical models of changes in advertising spend and changes in overall sales report a weak association. But if we look below the surface and divide the consumers who were exposed to the advertising from those who are not, then we can see sales effects that were previously masked. The value of individual-level data is illustrated in Figure 9.1, where the data shows that despite declining sales (because of competitive pressure) the brand's advertising really was generating purchases among those consumers who saw the ad.

Figure 9.1: Brand purchasing households, per dollars/1000 households

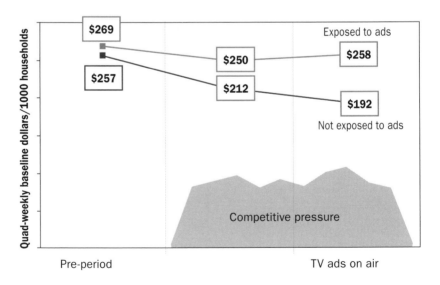

Source: Flaherty, 2007.

When rigorous controls of other causal influences on sales are in place (e.g. Danaher, Bonfrer & Dhar, 2008), advertising's effects appear greater, as we would expect; however, with aggregate data this is fiendishly difficult to do, making it astonishingly hard to see advertising's sales effects.

This is a difficult concept to grasp because it seems counter-intuitive—advertising causes sales even when sales figures don't change. When sales figures do change, this still gives an incorrect indication of the true effect advertising has on sales. Movements in this week's or month's sales figures don't reveal the sales impact of advertising—they are like the tip of the iceberg but we don't know what proportion of the total iceberg the tip represents.

This isn't always the case; for some advertising, the effect on sales occurs immediately. An example of this is the advertising that informs its audience of a time-dependent event, for example, 'Sale ends this Thursday'.[3] But most advertising affects people who won't buy the brand for weeks, so the sales effects are spread far into the future. Hence, the effect on sales is spread so thinly over a week's sales figures, that a change in weight of advertising delivers no visible change in sales trajectory. Broadbent (1989) provides an apt analogy of this, 'The sales of a brand are like the height at which an airplane flies. Advertising spend is like its engines: while the

---

3   Advertising with very strong 'recency' effects—this is in categories where buyers show very little interest until they actively start searching; for example, mortgages, insurance, furniture, computers and cars. In these categories, when consumers are not ready to buy they screen out much advertising; but, shortly before they do buy, they become dramatically more receptive to advertising. Thus advertising in these categories has a more immediate effect. An equally good way of describing this is to say that it has less of a longer term effect (little effect on buyers not ready to buy yet). However, even in these categories there is occasionally advertising that does break through and reach people who are not yet ready to buy. So it would be wrong to judge the sales effectiveness of this advertising purely according to how much sales increased that week—its sales effects are spread out way into the future when the exposed buyers finally buy from the category. Such advertising can be particularly sales effective, yet it may be no better than average at affecting a week's sales figures. It's the sort of advertising that is entertaining enough to grab people's attention who are not yet 'in the market'; for example, Apple's 'I'm a Mac, I'm a PC' and HSBC's 'different perspectives' advertisements.

engines are running everything is fine, but when the engines stop, the descent *eventually* starts'.

How advertising and price promotions cause sales in different ways

Chapter 4 discussed how all brands, even very large ones, mostly have very light (i.e. very occasional) buyers (see Figures 4.1, 4.2 and 4.3). We saw that most Coca-Cola buyers only buy themselves a Coke once or twice a year. At the other end of the spectrum, there is a tiny portion of consumers who buy Coke every morning, noon and night. Consider what happens to the buying behaviour of a person who drinks Coke several times a day after seeing a Coca-Cola ad—nothing changes. So who is Coke's advertising aimed at? It's aimed at the millions of people who occasionally buy Coca-Cola, who scarcely ever think of Coke and who seldom buy it. These consumers could easily forget about it and not make their semi-annual purchases. This is why established brands need to advertise: to hold onto their buyers (in the face of substantial competitor advertising) and to give themselves a chance to grow. Coke's advertising tries to grab a tiny window of our attention and remind us that Coke is fun, that we've had it before and we like it—Coke's advertisements are mostly reminding us of things we already know. By doing this, Coke is trying to increase our (very low) probability of buying it tomorrow. If it works, it changes our probability of buying tomorrow from almost nothing (say one chance in 300) to slightly more than almost nothing (say two chances in 300). This is a change in probability that is so slight we'd hardly notice, which is why people say that advertising doesn't affect them, because it's too subtle for them to notice. But if every person who is exposed to a single Coca-Cola ad increases his or her buying propensity from 1 chance in 300 to 2 chances in 300, Coke's sales among this group double![4] Therefore, even advertising that says nothing persuasive and gives no new reasons to buy

---

4   Of course, other people have been hit by competitor advertising and other influences, so this powerful advertising can still not show up in aggregate sales shifts.

can have a dramatic impact on sales—without causing people to rethink their opinion of a brand, and largely without them even noticing.

This explains why established brands have to spend considerable sums on advertising—the bigger the brand the more they have to spend, even if they are old and well known. It also explains why consumers often say they don't believe they are affected by advertising. In addition, it accounts for why advertising's sales effects show up in sales figures in a very different way than price promotions do. Put simply, the entire sales effect of a price promotion shows up in a week's sales figures, while the sales effect of advertising is spread very thinly into the future; this makes changes in advertising weight very difficult to see and extraordinarily hard to measure reliably.

Any marketing intervention, if it succeeds, works by increasing the probability that customers will purchase a product. Successful advertising reaches and affects many consumers; it reaches all types of consumers, not just the ones who are easy to reach (i.e. a brand's heavy, regular buyers, who easily notice the brand's advertising because their brand-related mental structures are better developed and they are less likely to screen out the advertising). Successful advertising, in particular, reaches the millions of consumers who have a very low probability of buying a brand next week or month. If a brand's advertising reaches them, if they notice it, if it refreshes, reinforces or builds the memory structures that make the brand more likely to be noticed or come to mind in a buying situation (i.e. enhancing brand salience and mental availability), then it nudges their propensity to buy the brand. This is the sales effect. But most of these additional sales won't show up in this week's sales figures because hardly any of these consumers will buy the brand this week; they simply don't buy that often even with their newly enhanced propensity. Indeed, most of these extra sales will never occur because, before the consumer even buys from the category, he or she will be hit with competitor advertising (or other marketing activity) that nullifies the effect of the advertising exposure. But this doesn't mean that the sales effect didn't happen; that nudge in propensity slightly protected the brand's sales from the effect of competitor activity. Instead of the competitor's ad winning extra sales it merely got the brand back to where it had been before.

Consider the people who, after being exposed to a Coke ad, increase their propensity to buy Coke tomorrow from 1 in 300 to 2 in 300. This means they will now make a purchase every 150 days, rather then once every 300 days. So these extra purchases take a long while to occur. This is the meaning of advertising's sales effects being spread thinly over time.

The reach of price promotions is very different. Their reach is very restricted as it's skewed to heavier, more regular buyers of a brand. Also, the sales effects of price promotions aren't spread out in time. In-store promotions only affect those people buying from the category in the week of the promotion. So the entire sales effect shows up in that week's sales figures. That's why price promotions show clear effects: sales increase when price promotions are turned on, and sales decrease when they are turned off.[5] There might be a longer lasting effect if purchasing and using the discounted brand leads to enhanced brand salience, but the evidence is that longer term effects of price promotions are minimal (see Chapter 10). Advertising's effect on purchase probability occurs through the effect on memories, and memories have some ability to last.[6] Whereas price discounts affect purchase probability because we like a better deal, if one of the brands that we use and notice is on sale then the chance leaps that we choose it over the other brands in our repertoire—but our purchase probabilities return to normal immediately afterwards. So the price discount only works while it is there.

That's great news for those seeking to measure the sales impact of price promotions (the full sales effect can be seen and measured in a week's sales figures), but it's sobering news for those seeking to measure the sales

---

5   Also the effect is easy to see because consumers' change in buying propensity is quite large, because we are spending quite a lot per consumer, whereas advertising spends very little per consumer, so its effect is a gentler nudge.

6   Indeed some memories created by advertising last forever. Their salience can fade, but they are always there and able to be refreshed. You'll never entirely forget that the Golden Arches mean McDonald's, that Google is a search engine and so on.

impact of advertising. It means you should never mix price promotion effects and advertising effects into a single econometric modelling attempt to quantify the relative sales effects of advertising and price changes.

However, the good news is that the sales response to advertising can be seen even when a market is stable and there is no aggregate level change in sales for the advertised brand. This requires what is known as 'single-source data': individual-level data that records continuously over time what each individual buys and what advertising they are exposed to. To explain the advantage of such data, consider how a direct marketer would assess the impact of a direct mail campaign to selected households in Chicago. Would they use national sales data? No. Would they use Chicago sales data? No. They would look at the buying patterns of the households they sent the letter to. No one expects sales to change in households that didn't get the letter. Also, to correctly estimate the real sales impact, the marketer would compare sales among these households against a benchmark, such as their prior buying history or the sales of similar households who were deliberately not sent the letter. Single-source data lets us employ the same logical approach to assessing the impact of television, print and other advertising (Kennedy, McDonald & Sharp, 2008; McDonald & Sharp, 2005).

Forty years of single-source-based analysis has delivered solid empirical evidence that advertising drives sales among those who are exposed to it (and that some advertisements are vastly better than others). These results have held across a range of brands, categories, countries and data sets (i.e. Jones, 1995a & b; McDonald, 1969; Roberts, 1994; Roberts, 1996; Roberts, 1998). This is good news for those who advertise. It is also good news for advertisers who want to measure the sales effects of their advertising so that they can work out what creative executions and what media strategies work better.

In a review of his single-source data analysis of sales effective advertising, Jones (1997) noted:

> The European styles of advertising ... understated, softness, quirkiness, indirectness, unusual visual effects, and bizarre humour ... are often

surprisingly effective. ... The advertising shown to have greatest effect ... were certainly not hard-selling in the conventional sense ... they were likeable ... visual rather than verbal.

Rather than examine in depth the findings of single-source research on advertising sales effects we will summarise the important findings that are supported by findings from other reliable methodologies, such as experiments:

- advertising generates sales
- some advertising copy is much more sales effective than others; some barely works at all
- creative copy without a persuasive message can still be very sales effective
- media strategy that achieves greater reach is particularly effective; reach is more important than frequency of exposure; continuous advertising is more effective than bursts followed by long gaps, because it counteracts memory decay.

All of this fits with the negative binomial distribution of buying rates (see Chapter 4). It particularly fits with the importance of reaching all category buyers, with solid coverage over time (i.e. no long gaps). Advertising works by reaching and nudging. This mostly happens without us noticing; occasionally an ad produces the reaction 'I should buy that' but even this intention only weakly nudges our buying propensities, because we often forget or are deflected from our intentions. This is a reminder that advertising works through its effect on memory.

Without noticing (and processing) there is nothing

An ad cannot build memory structures if it is not processed; memory structures cannot generate sales if they are not associated with the brand that is being advertised. Most advertising exposures fail these two hurdles, so the money spent is wasted, or worse, the ad refreshes memories for competitor brands. As discussed in Chapter 1, less than 20% of television advertisements are noticed and correctly branded (i.e. there is over 80% wastage). This is shocking; it's alarming enough to think that large corporations would have a special task force, perhaps within marketing, that was charged with eradicating this problem. This task force would conduct research and development, set guidelines and cultivate techniques for developing and evaluating advertising to ensure that all a brand's advertising passed these two hurdles. Yet the reality in most organisations is that these metrics are sometimes not even measured, no-one's job depends on them, and no-one is responsible for fixing the problem. Therefore, no serious research and development is allocated to the issue— think how different this would be if the issue were wastage in the factory or product failures.

It's true that advertising can work without us paying it much attention. We are able to notice things at a very low, even subconscious, level; for example, while in conversation at a crowded party we can still hear our name being called in the hubbub of background conversations. But just because part of our brain is monitoring our environment at a very low level, it doesn't mean that it lets this information impinge much on our long-term memories. It's better if advertising can generate more conscious attention and processing.

As people screen out so much advertising, the challenge is to get past the brain's screening mechanisms and to generate that little emotional reaction in the direction of acceptance: 'I will pay attention to this'. Therefore, the primary task of advertising agencies is to generate outstanding creative ideas that viewers will notice and will be willing to process over and over. This processing must be brand-centric; it must refresh the memory structures that relate to the brand. This is a difficult task, which is why most advertising fails. It's also why some of the new findings from neuroscience and psychology are so important—we need to understand how attention and memories work.

We now know that very little thinking, if any, can be described as purely rational. Emotion is a primary source of human motivation, and exerts substantial influence on attention, memory and behaviour; it is no wonder it is heavily used in advertising. For example, emotion can be seen in advertising when the audience sheds a tear watching an ad for cancer research, or laughs with the characters in a beer ad, or shows shock, fear and relief watching an insurance ad. People watch movies, listen to music and read books largely for an emotional ride. They enjoy gaining the same from advertising and when they get it they pay more attention.

Memory is everything

Apart from a very small amount of direct-response advertising (including online search engine advertising), advertising must work through memories. This is an uncontroversial statement, yet it is common for marketers and academics to forget the essential role of memory; instead, they think advertising works largely through persuasive arguments or by creating emotional feelings about a brand.

Memory is the link between an ad and brand choice. Even a frequently purchased item (e.g. margarine) is only bought, on average, eight times a year, and any single brand is only typically bought once or twice a year (Nielsen, 2007). There can be many months between exposure to an ad and when the viewer is in a shopping situation with a relevant opportunity to recall brand memories (which are possibly influenced by the ad). To influence behaviour, advertising must work with people's memories.

Building brand salience

The dominant way that advertising works is by refreshing, and occasionally building, memory structures. These structures improve the chance of a brand being recalled and/or noticed in buying situations; this in turn increases the chance of a brand being bought. Memory structures that relate to a brand include what the brand does, what it looks like, where it is available, when and where it is consumed, by who and with whom. Memories are associations with cues that can bring a brand to mind. They can also remind consumers to take it out of their pantry and eat it.

Persuading consumers

Some advertising creates an intention to purchase by gaining a reaction like 'I should buy that' or 'That's interesting, I really must check that out'. Some persuasive messages are very dry and rational; for example, classified advertising, directory advertising, new product advertising, newspapers and brochures. Typically, directory and classified advertising is informative, concise and organised according to the interests of the audience. For example, plumber X guaranteeing a visit within the day to your area might be all the persuasion you need when your hot water system blows. However, to persuade consumers to buy a new product, the market needs to be informed of what is on offer. The excitement of something new provides a window of opportunity: there is enough inherent emotion that an ad (that provides rational information) may get noticed.

However, persuasive arguments are more powerful if they include explicit emotional appeals. For example, compare these two appeals:

a Goodyear tyres grip the road and reduce your stopping distance.
b Today your child's life may depend on your braking ability. Goodyear tyres reduce your stopping distance and keep your loved ones safe.

Persuasive advertising occurs less than advertising texts and models would have us believe. Also, great sales-effective advertising does not need to persuade. We conducted a series of UK studies on the forms that advertisements take (FAT) (Mills, 2000) where the general public, agency professionals and students assessed television and magazine ads. Only 40–50% of the assessments thought the ads suggested or claimed that their brand was different or better, or provided helpful information. We suggest that in these cases there is no simple basis on which these ads could successfully persuade. Others (Morgan, Appiah-Adu & Ling, 1995) have also noted that most advertisements contain very little verbal or visual information about the advertised brand.

The persuasion mechanism does not explain most of the advertising in the world. Many brands are already successful. They do not have anything to say that the market does not already know, that a competitor could not say or is meaningful to their buyers. Yet it's commonly assumed that persuasion-oriented advertising must be more sales effective, but this is not true. Memory structures, even if they don't result in intentions, still cause sales—decades of research (e.g. Juster, 1960) shows that most sales typically come from people who had no intention of buying. Intentions are memories too, and subject to faulty recall so they are only weakly motivational. A similar point can be made about brand preference or attitude. Some advertising generates a reaction like 'that's good' or 'that would suit me'. Again, it is commonly assumed that such persuasive advertising must be more effective in generating sales.[7] Such attitudes are usually very weakly motivational. This is partly because they are not often recalled in buying situations and also because we often have a large number of brands we like (and that we buy).

So it is quite misplaced to conclude that advertising that affects intentions or attitudes works better. This fact undermines much academic research into advertising that has derived rules about effectiveness by examining the effect of advertising exposure on stated intentions (often in artificial laboratory settings with unrealistic lags and heightened attention). Similarly, advertising pre-tests (copy tests) that use intentions or intention shift are biased towards particular types of advertising content, and very often reach incorrect conclusions about the sales effectiveness of particular commercials.

Many companies are trapped in the intentions/preference paradigm. They brief their agencies and evaluate their advertising in line with this model (sometimes without even realising it). Consequently, they produce

---

7   Some writers, particularly in the US, think persuasion is synonymous with sales effectiveness. This is confusing and leads to the tautological statement that only persuasive advertising can generate sales.

advertising filled with persuasive arguments (often about trivial benefits) that are rejected, misunderstood or ignored by viewers. They also produce advertising that fails to refresh or build appropriate mental structures because management's attention is on the selling message. Such advertising fails to communicate consistently the distinctive aspects of a brand. Consequently, many firms produce campaign after campaign where each looks and feels different—as if each were for a different brand.

Somewhat ironically, companies that use this model of how advertising works will sometimes produce what they call 'image advertising' or 'awareness advertising', yet they do not expect this to produce sales. Of course it should be expected to generate sales—that's what advertising is for.

In summary, advertising largely works by refreshing memory structures; occasionally it also builds memory structures and creates a preference or an intention to purchase. Advertising maintains and builds brand salience via creative publicity. Brands don't need to worry about having a persuasive message; even when they have one, the message needs to be embedded within a framework of brand links and cues, salience and long-term distinctiveness.

Marketers need to understand the memory structures that have already been built for their brand. They need to use these, and ensure their advertising refreshes these structures. Then they need to research what other memory structures might be useful to the brand (i.e. factors driving purchase in the category) and then work to build these. Over decades, leading brands have done stellar jobs at building relevant memory structures. Coke is a great example. In the past, Coke was sold in US 'drug stores' and so it was associated with drug store visits in summer by teenagers. Today Coke is associated with a variety of memories: the beach and Coke, nightclubs and Coke, pizza and Coke, parties and Coke, cafés and Coke ('the original long black'), the Coke bottle, Coke red, Coke swirl and so on. These memories make it more likely that Coke will come to mind; they make it easier for people to notice Coke and to process Coke's advertising.

Other ways advertising can work

As discussed, there are two main ways that advertising works: persuasion (changing opinions) and salience (refreshing and building memories). There are other mechanisms, but these are more subtle and are often secondary to salience and/or persuasion. These other mechanisms include bond, status signals and priming, which are discussed below.

Bond

Spending money on advertising signals that a company is financially secure and/or their products are good, which is particularly important for services. Corporate reputation advertising is a prime example. The practice of spending large amounts of money on employing top celebrities to appear in ads, or sponsoring large events like the Olympics, is explained by this mechanism. Some consumers infer, perhaps subconsciously, that an advertiser would not foolishly spend lots of money on advertising if it did not have confidence in its product and did not intend to be around for a long time. Also, consumers' experience has taught them that heavily advertised products and services tend to be good quality.

Economists have supported this idea by arguing that the amount spent on advertising often seems more important than the message in determining the commercial outcome (i.e. Nelson, 1974; Telser, 1964). This does not mean that advertising has no economic function or that viewers are irrational; rather, viewers respond to signals beyond the explicit messages.

The economist John Kay (1993) asserts that most people are inherently cynical about truth in advertising and that they automatically discount claims about quality made in advertisements that cannot be objectively assessed. In this circumstance, he argues (exaggerating somewhat), the only thing advertising can convey is the quality and quantity of the advertising itself.

Status signals

When we use some brands we signal to others, and even to ourselves, what sort of person we are. Advertising helps this signalling. Few people drive a Mercedes-Benz, but everyone knows this is an expensive car brand. Advertising tells us this, which means that people who drive Mercedes signal their wealth by driving this brand. This wouldn't work if the general population didn't know what a Mercedes looks like and know that it is an expensive brand.

However, marketers often over-estimate the effect of signalling. Some categories aren't very symbolic, and some consumers think a brand will change what their friends think of them. Also, much of the symbolic character of brands comes from usage, observation and word of mouth rather than from advertising.

The implication of this is not that a brand will benefit enormously from advertising that tries to make it cool. A more sensible implication is that symbolic brands and even super expensive luxury brands often need to advertise widely. Advertising for luxury watches is not just directed towards billionaires, partly because most people aren't billionaires and most people who buy luxury watches aren't billionaires.

Priming

It is a well-established psychological phenomenon that people prefer objects and brands that they have seen more often. This is an 'exposure' effect. Recent research has shown that this effect can apply to exposures that consumers are barely aware of. Research has also revealed that recent exposures to associated cues can enhance the probability of purchase. For example, college students returning to campus after Halloween rated orange brands more favourably and exposure to multiple pictures of dogs increased the probability of choosing the Puma brand of sports shoes (because people associate dogs with cats) (Berger & Fitzsimons, 2008). This extraordinary effect isn't well documented outside of experimental conditions, so it's unclear how strong this effect really is in the real world. It is also not clear how competing cues interact and possibly cancel each other out. It's possible that this exposure effect is simply a salience effect. This is further evidence that advertising can affect sales without making a sales pitch.

Effective advertising

A simple recipe for effective advertising is:

- reach all the category buyers
- don't have long lapses in advertising
- get noticed, not screened out, by consumers
- use clear brand links—a brand's distinctive assets indirectly brand advertising; mentioning (verbally and/or visually) the brand name is crucial; showing the product and showing the product in use is important
- refresh and build memory structures that make a brand more likely to come to mind and be easier to notice
- if there is a piece of information that is genuinely persuasive, then say it, so long as it does not interfere with achieving the previous objectives.

10

What Price Promotions Really Do

John Dawes & John Scriven

Price promotions have an immediate and positive effect on sales. But the effect does not last; it ends when the price discount ends. This is because price promotions largely reward customers who have bought the discounted brand in the past (and who are lucky enough to find it on sale). Price promotions do not alter underlying propensities to buy in the future; they lack reach and usually fail to bring new customers to a brand.

Introduction

A book about the laws of marketing and buying behaviour would not be complete without discussing price. This chapter reveals the law-like patterns in how consumers react to price changes, particularly how temporary price discounts affect buying, sales and profits.

Price is not all-important

Price is a powerful variable in the marketing mix. It is arguably the easiest element of a product to change and it has the largest direct effect on sales. Price obviously matters to consumers, and is often thought to be the most important factor. Yet, brand leaders are almost never the cheapest. Not all buyers switch when a more expensive brand becomes cheaper. Therefore, price is not everything. So how do consumers react to price and to price changes and why do they behave as they do?

This chapter principally comments on what happens when the price of an established brand is changed temporarily, for example, in a price promotion. We will not be discussing the process of setting a price. However, it is important to bear in mind that each brand has a 'normal' price that reflects the quality of the brand. Most categories have price/quality tiers: the cheap/basic, no-added-frills level; the mainstream level; and the level of higher priced products that have added luxury or functionality. Consumers are aware of this tier system, so considering context is important when evaluating the prices people are willing to pay. It is apparent that consumers will pay for quality: the prices for higher quality brands are higher than the prices for lower quality brands, and the higher quality brands do well year after year. We also see that, generally, the very best brands are considerably more expensive, and the very cheapest brands are often considerably lower quality—if you really want quality, you have to pay for it.

We will now examine these questions: How do consumers behave in relation to price? Are there 'deal buyers' and 'premium buyers'? We will also outline the managerial motivation for running price promotions and reveal what actually happens when price promotions are run. The question of longer-term effects (good or bad) is also addressed. Finally, we will discuss the capacity of price promotions to actually reach buyers.

Consumers buy across a range of price levels

Marketers and researchers find it tempting to categorise shoppers according to the prices they pay. For example, it is thought that there are low-end shoppers, those who buy in the middle range and others who buy premium products. The notion of the 'deal-prone' shopper reinforces this view. However, research into actual buying behaviour shows that consumers do not confine themselves to one price category. Most consumers buy across a range of prices—over time they will buy the same brand at different prices and also buy brands that sit at different prices. This might be because of availability, promotions, something catching their eye, differing needs, mood swings, wanting a change, granny coming to visit and so on. These many random influences result in law-like patterns in cross-buying at different price levels. For example, Table 10.1 shows that in the instant coffee market in the UK about half (51%) those buying in the cheapest price range (denoted as '- -') also bought in the most expensive price range ('+ +'). Similarly, of those buying in the below-average price range ('-'), 57% also bought in the most expensive price range, and so on. Overall, these patterns are dictated by the number of people who buy in each price range, much like the double jeopardy law for brand buying described in Chapter 2. That is, people who buy in any price tier will also buy in other price tiers, in line with how big those other price tiers are.

Table 10.1: Buying in different price tiers: instant coffee in a year

Buyers of		Share	Percentage buying in other price tiers			
			-	- -	++	+
Below average	–	35		64	57	36
Cheap	– –	31	69		51	30
Expensive	++	27	66	55	–	39
Above average	+	7	78	61	73	–
Average		**25**	**71**	**60**	**60**	**35**

Notes: • Rows and Columns are ordered by popularity of the price tier.
  • Buyers of any price tier also buy in other price tiers, about in line with the market share of those other price tiers

Source: TNS.

What this means is that if you manage a 'low price' brand, the people who buy it aren't dedicated to only purchasing lower priced brands; many of your sales actually come from people who normally buy mid-range and premium brands, and who sometimes buy a cheap one. The same is true for premium brands—many sales actually come from the 'low price' buyers who occasionally buy a higher priced brand. So in any particular market, there are consumers who habitually buy a range of brands and pay a range of prices. It is therefore hard to successfully target an exclusively 'low price buyer' segment with price promotions, because such a segment doesn't usually exist.

Why do managers run price promotions?

According to marketing texts, brand managers should build and manage brands by following these steps:

1 assess customer needs and the competitive situation
2 construct an offering and brand positioning that will resonate with buyers
3 set a price that reflects the value of the brand to the buyer.

What happens in practice is that brands are routinely discounted below their normal price to generate a short-term increase in sales. Sometimes more than half a brand's sales are made at the discounted price. This raises the question of which of the two price levels is the normal price for the brand.

What is the purpose of generating these short-term sales spikes? In many cases they do not deliver extra profit, because the margin given away on sales would have been made anyway, at full price.

Price promotions are popular with managers because the results are easy to see. More stock is sold. If a brand is sold through retailer outlets, sales tracking immediately shows an impressive spike. The immediacy is attractive. This may be important for a company that needs to transform inventory into money. There are other related reasons—such as managers being under pressure to make unit sales budgets. Price promotions deliver these results, but they also lead to volume targets that require more price discounting. Price promotions can become a way of life for organisations because winding them back would result in failing to hit sales targets.

Therefore, such promotions are highly addictive for marketers. Another reason for the popularity of these discounts is that distribution channels (such as retailers) demand them, because a retailer can then offer discounts to consumers and build an image of good value. Discounts at the retail level also allow a retailer to maintain competitive pressure on its rivals. Therefore, price promotions on the part of manufacturers can be one of the costs of maintaining good relationships with retail distributors. Unfortunately, in-store promotions empower the distributor because the market share of the brand becomes dependent on the distributor's decisions. Price promotions can also 'buy time' for a brand—boost sales in the short term or save it from being delisted. However, something must be done while the clock is ticking, and there is evidence that more emphasis on price promotions is accompanied by lower emphasis on innovation (Pauwels et al., 2004). Finally, it may be that price promotions are so popular because it is hard to think of more creative ideas for brand strategy.

Price promotions don't win new customers

Some marketers believe that price cuts attract new customers to buy a brand: customers who might later make more purchases at full price. However, there is little evidence this occurs. Ehrenberg, Hammond and Goodhardt (1994) found that almost everyone who bought a brand during a price promotion had bought the brand previously. Some academic researchers have even found that some sales in a price promotion have been brought forward from future sales, so the spike in volume at the time of the sale is cancelled out to some degree because of lower sales post promotion. Fortunately, the evidence is that the main effect is brand substitution, not forward buying.

If price promotions can't attract new buyers, can they at least bring back infrequent buyers? Perhaps the acts of purchase and use could reinforce infrequent buyers' propensity to buy again. This possibility has been investigated as the 'purchase reinforcement effect'. What has been found is that a price promotion pulls in a large proportion of infrequent buyers (i.e. buyers who have a low propensity to buy a brand). They buy during the promotion and then afterwards resume their very low buying propensity. In other words, after the promotional purchase it is as if nothing happened. Why is this the case? Let's think about consumers' purchases over a long period. They may have purchased that category dozens or hundreds of times before. Buying this brand on deal is nothing special to consumers; they have bought that brand before, just as they have bought competitor brands before, either on special or at normal price. Now let us consider what might occur before these infrequent buyers purchase from the category again. Ehrenberg's work over decades shows that the incidence of category purchasing follows a negative binomial distribution (NBD): lots of infrequent buyers and a few frequent buyers (Ehrenberg, 1959; Goodhardt, Ehrenberg & Chatfield, 1984). So for the majority of buyers, a lot of time may elapse before they buy from that particular category again. While the elapsed time between purchases may only be a week or two for some buyers in some categories (e.g. regular milk or bread buyers), it could be several months for instant coffee or toothpaste and six months to a year for less regularly purchased goods. When the time does come for customers to re-buy from the category in question, they may have purchased dozens of brands in a range of other categories. Some of those purchases will have been on special, some not. This means that the act of buying any one particular brand on promotion in any one particular category will easily be forgotten before the next time. Buying brands that are temporarily promoted is a routine, very frequent behaviour for consumers. There is little scope for a permanent or semi-permanent behavioural change. In summary, what price promotions do (for established brands) is to jolt the short-term buying propensities of mainly infrequent buyers who take the opportunity to buy the brand cheaply and then resume their normal purchase behaviour afterwards (i.e. to buy it sometimes as part of a wider repertoire). As Pauwels, Hanssens and Siddarth (2002, p. 437) state, 'Price promotions produce only temporary benefits for established brands.'

Negative after-effects

Many marketers are justifiably worried about the possible negative after-effects of price promotions. Such after-effects include consumer resistance to paying normal price after purchasing at a discounted price; this is a manifestation of the 'reference price effect'. A number of studies have found reference price effects (e.g. Hardie, Johnson & Fader, 1993; Lattin & Bucklin, 1989) in grocery markets. However, another stream of research on price knowledge has found that many consumers struggle to recall the prices they paid for goods (Vanhuele & Drèze, 2002). How can there be a reference price effect if consumers have a low level of price recall and buying brands on special is routine? Let's tackle this paradox by reviewing the reference price research and the studies on price recall, and then reconcile the results from both research streams.

Reference price

The academic research on pricing emphasises the notion of a consumer reference price—especially the consumer's internal reference price, which is a memory or expectation of what prices should be (note: the concept of an external reference price refers to information on the prices of alternatives). This expectation of price is thought to be generated by exposure to prices in the past, either by purchasing or observing communications such as ads. The idea of a reference price is that 'past prices matter' and if consumers encounter a price above their reference price, this dampens their propensity to buy. Analysis of consumer panel data has found that purchasing on deal in the past has a dampening effect on purchasing at normal price in the future.

Price knowledge

We have to reconcile the notion of a reference price effect with consumers' less-than-perfect knowledge about prices and the routine nature of shopping described above. Many studies of consumers' ability to recall prices have shown their recall to be poor. In the US, a large-scale study (Dickson & Sawyer, 1990) was conducted in which shoppers were intercepted shortly after selecting a product; of these shoppers, only about half knew the price of the item they selected to within 5%. In France, the figure was about a third of shoppers (Vanhuele & Drèze, 2002). It seems that either the memory trace for the price of the item was very momentary, or that little attention was paid to the price of the item in the first place. In the Dickson and Sawyer study, many shoppers claimed they did not check the price of the item or check the prices of alternatives.

The initial findings about consumers' price knowledge, such as the 1990 Dickson and Sawyer (1990) study, were based on price recall. More recently, researchers have argued that two other measures are more appropriate: recognition and deal spotting. Recognition studies show shoppers three prices for an item that are (for example) the normal price, 10% above the normal price and 10% below the normal price. Vanheule and Dreze (2002) applied this approach to consumers, and found that only 13% of shoppers identified the correct price. This suggests that price recognition is also rather poor. In terms of deal spotting, approximately 50% of shoppers have a good ability to spot a 'good deal' for a particular brand based on being shown a price for it; the other half have some difficulty knowing if a particular price for an item is a good price.

The conclusion is that while consumers' knowledge about prices is hazy, an appreciable proportion of consumers has a fair idea about price within a zone of the actual price. Also, consumers do seem to be aware of relativities between brands (i.e. X is usually more expensive than Y), rather than absolute price levels, and that comparison between available brands is more important.

So, will a temporary price promotion have negative after-effects for a brand? The answer is no, but repetitively doing it may have negative after-effects. This is because if consumers commonly encounter low prices and 'deal' signals for a brand, their reference price for it will be lowered. Also, customers will get used to seeing price-related information for the brand, which will raise the salience of price and possibly lower the salience of other important brand attributes. US studies (Mela, Gupta & Lehmann, 1997; Mela, Jedidi & Bowman, 1998) found that more frequent promotions result in heightened sensitivity to price among consumers, as well as slightly longer interpurchase times and slightly higher purchase quantities. That is, consumers learn to not only buy on deal, but to also buy a little more during the price promotion, which results in less frequent purchases.

In terms of long-term adverse effects, competitive retaliation is another factor to consider. Managers tend to over-react to each other's price reductions (Brodie, Bonfrer & Cutler, 1996). More broadly, competitor response to price has been shown to be less than rational, with some firms placing more emphasis on 'beating the competition' with low prices than on pursuing profit. Companies that do this tend to depress their profits (Armstrong & Collopy 1996). An interesting example of the destructive potential of a 'beat the competition' mentality is the price war between Greyhound and Peter Pan Trailways (Heil & Helsen, 2001 p. 86). The price of a bus fare went from $25 to $9.95 to $7 to $6.95, and then Greyhound offered a $4 fare, which was lower than the price it had charged 40 years previously. This rapid, ruinous price descent took place over a short period of three weeks. In extreme cases, price wars can bankrupt multiple players. Therefore, a decision to engage in discounting, or to escalate it, must consider that competitors are likely to respond in kind, which will result in lower profits, or even severe hardship, for all players.

How much extra volume does a price cut generate?

Price promotions boost sales volume in the short term; but by how much? The term used to discuss this is price 'elasticity'—the percentage change in volume from a 1% change in price. For example, if a price is cut by 10% and sales volume increases by 20%, the elasticity is −2 (20/10 = 2, the minus indicates that price and volume move in opposite directions).

Studies have found a reasonable degree of consistency in the average elasticity for temporary promotions. Danaher and Brodie (2000, p. 923) found an average price elasticity of −2.3 across 26 categories, with almost all the price changes examined being for temporary promotions. Scriven and Ehrenberg (2004) found an average elasticity of −2.6 in an exhaustive series of experiments that included both price increases and decreases. Steenkamp and colleagues (2005) examined 442 product categories and reported a mean elasticity of −4.0. Summaries of in-market studies have found an average price elasticity of −2.5 (Bijmolt, van Heerde & Pieters, 2005; Tellis, 1988).

These results suggest that on average we can expect an increase in sales volume of approximately 25% from a 10% price cut. Most of the authors cited above point out that individual elasticity can vary greatly from 0 to −20 or bigger, although the majority, 70% or so, fall in the range just smaller than −1 to −4. Scriven and Ehrenberg shed light on this variation, showing that elasticity is not a fixed property of a brand, but varies systematically with the context in which a choice decision is made. They found five factors consistently led to bigger price elasticities, which are now explained.

Factors leading to bigger price elasticities

1 If the brand's price moves past a local 'reference price'

People are more likely to switch from brand A to brand B when B becomes cheaper than A (where previously, B was more expensive). Changing relative price positions is far more effective than just narrowing the price gap. Similarly, widening a price gap that already exists has less effect than changing relative positions. Also, the larger competitor brand B is, the bigger the effect. Therefore, setting the price of a brand slightly below that of the biggest brands in the category may be a better tactic than either deeply undercutting the leaders' prices, or setting the price close to the leader's price, but not undercutting it.

2 If the price change is explicitly signalled

Signalling the price change has a big effect. The signalling effect links to the notion that consumers have imperfect awareness of prices and their relativities. Therefore, if we draw attention to a price cut (e.g. 'was $54 now $30'), more people will be aware of the price and act on it. Also, of course, consumers like a bargain. Many studies of the effect of in-store price signals such as signage and displays can result in massive, short-term gains in sales. If a price cut is accompanied by in-store advertising, sales can increase by as much as 400% (Woodside & Waddle, 1975). In the UK, Hamilton, East and Kalafatis (1997) reported that price cuts coupled with additional promotional support can increase sales by around 200–500%. Totten and Block (1994, p. 70) reported that a deep price cut of 45%, supported by feature or display advertising, can increase sales by approximately 280% and possibly as much as 400%.

3   If the brand's share is low

Big brands have smaller price elasticities; small brands have bigger elasticities. This is an arithmetic effect, a result of elasticity being calculated using percentages. It is easy to imagine a brand moving from a 2% to a 6% market share (e.g. with a 50% price cut, this would require an elasticity of −4). The same elasticity and price cut on a brand with a 30% market share could enlarge the brand's share to 90%, which is almost impossible to achieve. This difference in elasticity means small brands can enjoy bigger uplifts from promotions, but suffer more than big brands when they increase prices. Conversely, bigger brands find it harder to get really big proportional sales rises from promotions, but suffer a little less than small brands when they put prices up.

4   If the price is increased from its normal level

It is often assumed that elasticity is the same for price rises as cuts, but there is no reason why this should be so. Empirical results from a series of experiments (Scriven & Ehrenberg, 2004) show that price increases have a bigger effect on volume than cuts do—if we consider the sole effect of a price change, divorced from extra effects of signalling or in-store support.

Larger price elasticities for price increases are consistent with a well-known finding in consumer psychology called 'loss aversion'. Experimental studies show support for loss aversion; for example, many consumers are reluctant to accept fair bets because the potential loss, of say $20, outweighs the attractiveness of possibly winning $20 (Kahneman & Tversky, 1979). If consumers have an approximate reference price for a brand, an increase above that reference level is perceived as a 'loss' with a corresponding drop in the likelihood of purchase.

This differential effect of price increases appears to be even more marked for private label brands: their downward price elasticity tends to be quite low (because they are already often cheaper), but if their price is put up, their sales loss is quite pronounced.

5 If the brand's normal price is close to the average of the other brands

If the price of a brand is close to the average prices of competitors, its elasticity will be greater. There are two reasons for this. First, if prices for all the brands are very dispersed, then a price change by one brand bridges the price gap between it and competitors by a smaller amount.

Second, if the brand's price is close to the average of competitors, a price change—either upward or downward—will take the brand past the price of one or more of those competitors (i.e. go from cheaper to dearer, or vice versa). Pricing experiments showed average price elasticities in double figures when all the brands start at the same price—because a change results in setting one brand's price below all the others, resulting in a huge swing in consumer choice. A good example of this phenomenon is petrol in urban locations where it is easy to switch from one station to another.

By contrast, elasticities are smaller when a brand's price is further away from the centre or average of the prices in its category. This dampening effect on price elasticity is especially marked if most of the other competitor brands' prices are close together.

There are three other category characteristics that lead to larger price elasticities. These are (1) categories with fewer brands, (2) goods that consumers buy very regularly and (3) categories that can be stockpiled (Narasimhan, Neslin & Sen, 1996).

Can price cuts be profitable?

An important point to make is that even very large increases in volume may still not make any extra contribution to profit. This is because, when a price is cut, the contribution margin[1] for each item is cut even more. For example, if the normal contribution margin on a product is 50%, a 10% price cut shaves 20% off the contribution margin. In the Totten and Block (1994) example (previously discussed), a price cut as reported of 45% would eliminate virtually all the contribution margin for a normal packaged goods brand; therefore, the brand is being sold at close to manufacturing cost. So while the brand could sell 400% more volume, it would not make any more profit, because there is almost no contribution margin on each item sold.

The short-term profitability of a price promotion depends on these three factors:

1 the contribution margin of the brand at normal price
2 the depth of the price cut
3 the price elasticity of the brand.

Using these three factors we can easily work out 'break-even' scenarios that show how much extra volume needs to be sold to break even from a price reduction. If the contribution margin is low to begin with, a massive increase in sales is needed to break even. If the contribution margin is high, a price cut can earn more profit, even from a modest increase in sales. This is because every extra unit still carries enough contribution to pay for the price cut. Three example scenarios are shown in Table 10.2. The first example shows that a brand selling at the normal price and earning

---

1   The contribution margin is the selling price, less variable costs. It is the amount 'left over' to cover fixed costs.

a 30% contribution margin and employing a 10% price cut must sell 50% more to just make the same amount of money. If the promotion creates an increase in sales of only 40%, the brand will lose money!

Table 10.2: Break-even scenarios

Price reduction (%)	For a brand with a 30% contribution margin at normal price	For a brand with a 40% contribution margin at normal price	For a brand with a 50% contribution margin at normal price
	Increase in sales needed to match the current contribution (%)	Increase in sales needed to match the current contribution (%)	Increase in sales needed to match the current contribution (%)
1	3	2	2
5	20	10	11
10	50	33	25
20	200	100	66

Such large increases in sales are needed because a price reduction results in selling lots of volume to people who would have bought the brand anyway, at full price. Therefore, the incremental volume has to be high to 'pay for' the lost margin on what we can call the baseline volume. This is illustrated in Figure 10.1. There are some obvious spikes in sales that are one-week price specials.

Note that the dark grey bars represent the baseline or normal level of sales that would have been made anyway if the price promotion had not occurred. These normal sales would have been sold at full price, not a discounted price.

Because the contribution margin is reduced by an exponentially increasing rate from larger discounts, the implication for managers employing price promotions is that they should make them as shallow as possible (e.g. 10% off, not 20% off). Even if this does not result in such high volume increases, at least the volume is making more contribution to profit.

Figure 10.1: Sales for a leading cereal brand

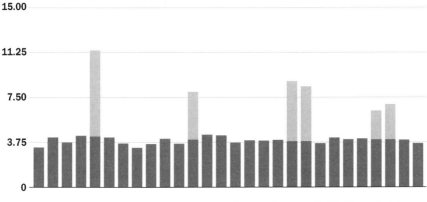

Source: Data supplied by Synovate Aztec.

There is one other factor that can impinge on the short-term profitability of a price promotion: unit sales may decline immediately afterwards. This can happen because the promotion has induced some consumers to accelerate their purchases. Empirical evidence suggests a trough can occur in sales after a promotion (Mace & Neslin, 2004; van Heerde, Leeflang & Wittink, 2000). If this happens, the promotion has borrowed some full-price, full-margin sales from the future; this dissipates its potential profitability. Managers should allow for this effect when evaluating promotions.

We now compare pricing with advertising as a means of stimulating demand (and maintaining marketplace position).

Comparing price versus advertising

Price cutting has a large, direct effect, but a very small reach. Advertising has great reach but a small direct effect at the level of the individual consumer. Advertising arguably also has a long-term effect, because it works on underlying propensities, whereas price promotion does not affect ongoing propensity and does not have favourable long-term effects.

It is certainly true that in-store price promotions are highly targeted: they only reach the buyers who are in the market for that category in that week. It would therefore seem they should be very efficient. However, this targeting through price promotions is very expensive—10% or 20% off the price of every item sold! Price cutting gives a lot away to people who would buy the brand anyway.

For manufacturers who sell through distribution channels, price promotions can occur with several levels of retailer support, and retailer support has implications for reach. The lowest level of support is an in-store price cut with only the ubiquitous 'special' ticket on shelf. An in-store price cut has the lowest level of reach, because only consumers who happen to be in the store and look at brands in the category at the time will notice it. The number of consumers who would do so in any given week comprise a very small proportion of the market. For example, in grocery markets, in a typical promotion period of two weeks, approximately 60% of households buy bread, 20% buy soup and 10% purchase a category such as shampoo—but these figures are the total penetration across all retailers. A price promotion in any one retailer will only reach a fraction of these buyers: given a retailer market share of say 10%, such a price promotion in that retailer will only reach 10% × 60% = 6% of bread buyers, 10% × 20% = 2% of soup buyers and 10% × 10% = 1% of shampoo buyers. So this sort of price promotion has very low reach.

The next level of in-store support involves an 'end-of-aisle' display. Nearly everyone in the store at the time could notice this display, but there is an upper limit on its reach, being the proportion of the population shopping in that retailer in that week—which is often a small proportion.

The third level of distributor support involves the brand being advertised in catalogues or through the retailer's mass media advertising. This takes the price promotion, and the brand, to a much broader audience. Arguably, the reach of this level of support is as large as the reach of mainstream advertising. However, advertising a price promotion so widely risks lowering the reference price for the brand to a wider group of people. Therefore, it might be preferable to organise an off-shelf display or retailer advertising without the price cut, but price-cutting is usually mandatory to obtain an off-shelf display or to feature in the retailer's advertising.

To summarise, the following observations have been made in this book:

a   Reach is important for brand growth.

b   In-store promotions generally lack reach, but retailer advertising has much broader reach.

c   Price promotions may not be profitable, particularly when the price cut is deep.

d   There is the possibility that reference prices would be eroded, particularly from deep price cuts.

However:

e   Manufacturers often feel pressurised to participate in price promotions.

Based on these observations, if a manufacturer had to choose between a promotion that emphasised deep price cuts or a promotion that focused on advertising the brand, the manufacturer should select the latter. This is because the brand would then feature in retailer advertising, which works more like normal advertising and attains reach for the brand. This communication may have to be linked to a reduced price, but the price need not be as low as it would be if the emphasis was all on price and less on communication support.

Conclusion

A price promotion will deliver an increase in sales in most cases. How large this sales increase is and whether the promotion is profitable depends on factors such as the size of the brand and what its price is relative to the competition before and after the price cut. Current evidence suggests there is no long-term increase in sales as a result of the spike in sales during the price promotion: buyers return to their pre-promotion buying patterns and sales return to pre-promotion levels. This means that a price promotion's effect on sales and profit can be easily evaluated—the analyst need only consider the sales spike during the promotion period, as well as any possible trough in sales immediately afterward.

In many cases, managers have other motives for running price promotions than just chasing sales spikes. A commonly cited reason for manufacturers to run promotions is to please or placate the retailer. In the long run this may be the only justifiable reason for price promotions, but if maintaining retailer relations is the objective of a price promotion then this should be the metric that is evaluated—yet such evaluation is seldom done in any formal sense.

To conclude, much price discounting is significantly costly: it erodes brand margins for the benefit of the retailer and consumer. The advice to brand owners is to think long and hard about what price-cutting activity is achieving in the long term, and try to reverse the long-term trend of marketing money being transferred from brand-building activities to discounting.

Why Loyalty Programs Don't Work

Byron Sharp

Loyalty programs are structured marketing efforts that reward, and therefore encourage, loyal buying behaviour. The most typical programs provide consumers with points when they make purchases. Gradually, after many purchases, these points add up and reach a level where they may be redeemed for rewards. This points system is an incentive for consumers to purchase a particular brand more frequently (i.e. increasing their loyalty) in order to gain more rewards faster. Such loyalty programs discourage defection from the brand as, once customers have accumulated points, and if they enjoy and value the loyalty program, they are less likely to defect to another brand.

Huge sums of money have been invested in loyalty programs over the past decade. Some marketers implemented these programs because it was fashionable to do so, or launched programs because they now had the technology to do so. However, most marketers were motivated by the hope that loyalty programs would improve loyalty. They anticipated great business results, with large increases in sales and profit.[1]

---

1   Authors such as Reichheld and Sasser (1990) had promised huge increases in profit from small improvements in loyalty (as discussed in Chapter 3).

However, as discussed in Chapter 1, marketing strategies that are based on false assumptions will never deliver high returns, no matter how well executed the strategies. The key assumptions that underpinned the large investments in loyalty programs are faulty. Many people assumed that loyalty levels could easily be dramatically improved; that customer defection could be reduced (to zero even); and that existing customers could be encouraged to devote all their purchasing to one brand (100% loyalty). It was assumed this would lead to substantial growth in revenue and profits. It was also mistakenly assumed that targeting a brand's most loyal customers would generate the greatest return. Enthusiasm for loyalty programs has now waned, and some firms are winding down loyalty programs. There is no evidence that outstanding business results are driven by loyalty programs.

Loyalty programs are still big business. One of the problems with large-scale consumer loyalty programs is that they are difficult for firms to exit from. Consumers who have accumulated points do not take kindly to losing them. If consumers are told they are losing their points, they tend to place an unrealistic, inflated value on the points—even if they were unlikely to redeem them. There are also contractual and legal impediments to shutting down a loyalty program, and there are the considerable sunk costs (including management ego) invested in the program. Firms turn out to be quite loyal to their loyalty programs, and tend to continue them far longer than rational economics would recommend.

Do loyalty programs work?

Do loyalty programs affect loyalty? You may be surprised to hear that yes, they do. However, the effect is very weak. The Ehrenberg-Bass Institute published the first large-scale empirical study (see Sharp & Sharp, 1997a) that analysed one of the world's largest (in terms of retail coverage) loyalty programs in Australia. The study observed a weak effect.

The technical difficulty in evaluating the effect of loyalty programs on loyalty is to have a baseline to make comparisons from. Simply comparing the behaviour of loyalty program members to non-members is inappropriate because a brand's more loyal customers will join the program (i.e. a selection effect because they have more to gain). Looking for changes in consumers' behaviour from when the loyalty program was implemented is difficult, because this requires having data on long periods of continuous purchasing before and after the implementation of the program.[2] Fortunately, the scientific laws introduced in this book mean that benchmarks are available for loyalty metrics; these are used to see if brands that ran loyalty programs have unusual loyalty for their market share.

Table 11.1 illustrates the results of the Ehrenberg-Bass Institute's study, which examined the cross-category loyalty program, FlyBuys[3] (FlyBuys is a separate program in two countries: Australia and New Zealand). Loyalty programs should make brands look niche, that is, their market share should be made up of unusually high loyalty and low penetration.[4] This is because loyalty programs reach a restricted element of the customer base and encourage these consumers to buy more frequently. Table 11.1 shows each brand in the FlyBuys loyalty program and the penetration and loyalty metrics necessary to make up its market share. By comparing the predicted and observed market share composition, we can see there does appear to be a loyalty effect. However, the effect is so weak that it isn't consistent; some brands don't show the pattern presumably because other marketing mix factors swamp the weak effect.

---

2   A long period of data is required to correctly classify the loyalty level of individual consumers because their buying fluctuates. The law of buyer moderation (see Chapter 4) means that many members of loyalty programs will be misclassified as less loyal than they really are; over time it will look as if these buyers are becoming more loyal and this 'regression to the mean' effect will be mistakenly attributed to the loyalty program. One analysis of a very small convenience store loyalty program suffered from this (Liu, 2007).

3   FlyBuys, as the name suggests, rewards shoppers with points that can be redeemed for flights.

4   The other sort of unusual market share a brand could have is unusually low loyalty and high penetration. This is occasionally seen for brands that many people buy but only on particular occasions (e.g. chocolate eggs at Easter).

Table 11.1: The FlyBuys loyalty program

Brand	Size of customer base Penetration (%)		Average purchase frequency		Loyalty-related Share of requirements (%)		Sole buyers (%)	
	Observed	Predicted	Observed	Predicted	Observed	Predicted	Observed	Predicted
Department stores (Australia)								
Kmart	48	52	3.7	3.4	34	31	10	7
Target	43	42	2.9	3.0	27	27	5	6
Myer	35	34	2.8	2.8	23	25	5	5
Supermarkets (Australia)								
Coles	61	64	9.8	9.4	31	29	5	3
Bilo	58	60	9.1	8.9	29	27	3	3
Retail petrol (Australia)								
Shell	46	51	6.3	5.8	42	35	11	10
Bank credit cards (NZ)								
NAB	20	25	9.6	7.2	87	70	79	63
BNZ	27	28	8.1	7.9	88	84	79	80
Phone calls (NZ)								
Telecom	86	85	24.8	24.7	94	93	88	87
Retail petrol (NZ)								
Shell	54	57	6.9	6.5	52	47	22	16
Average	**48**	**50**	**8.4**	**8.0**	**51**	**47**	**31**	**28**

Professors Lars Meyer-Waarden and Christophe Benavent (2006) replicated the Ehrenberg-Bass FlyBuys analysis using the AGB BehaviorScan panel in France. They examined the effect of four supermarket loyalty programs and they too observed weak and inconsistent effects. Leenheer and colleagues (2007) used a different approach (a one-off statistical model) to control selection effects (i.e. that the most loyal consumers join a brand's loyalty program). Their study of Dutch supermarket loyalty programs also found very small loyalty effects. Another Dutch researcher (Verhoef, 2003) found small, positive effects on retention and share in the financial services market; however, Verhoef acknowledged that the longitudinal design of his study didn't fully account for the selection effects. It is a consistent story. Loyalty programs produce very slight loyalty effects, and do practically nothing to drive growth. The consequent effect on profits is presumably negative.

Why don't loyalty programs work better?

The answer lies in the fact that from a marketing strategy perspective there is something unusual about loyalty programs: they skew, more than other marketing interventions, towards heavier, more loyal buyers of the brand. This selection effect occurs for two reasons. The first is physical and mental availability: it is easier for more loyal buyers to notice the loyalty program and to join. This is particularly true of retail loyalty programs where usually the only way of joining is to sign up in-store; more regular shoppers have a statistically higher chance of joining due to chance exposure. The second reason is the economic incentive to join, which is much stronger for already loyal buyers who can see that they will be rewarded for doing what they already do—getting 'something for nothing' is an attractive deal.

Essentially, consumers who rarely buy a brand (or shop in a particular store) don't see the loyalty program—and if they do they can't see the point in joining. This substantially restricts the reach of loyalty programs, and hence limits their capacity to drive substantial growth. There is also the question of what effect the loyalty program has on those consumers who it does reach (i.e. consumers who join the program and remember to participate). Logically, this effect will not only depend on the strength of the loyalty program, but also on which particular consumers the loyalty program recruits. Table 11.2 shows that there are four types of consumers a loyalty program can recruit and potentially influence (i.e. influence their loyalty towards the brand with the loyalty program).

Table 11.2: Types of customers who could join the loyalty program

		Level of loyalty	
		Low	**High**
Category purchase rate	**Light**	Unlikely to join the program (but this is the largest group of consumers, so a number still do join); not particularly desirable	Likely to join the program, but undesirable
	Heavy	Very unlikely to join the program, but very desirable	Likely to join the program, but undesirable

Most consumers fall into the top left-hand quadrant because most buyers are lighter-than-average consumers (of products in a particular category) and most of a brand's buyers also buy other brands.[5] A loyalty program will inevitably recruit some of these light consumers because there are so many of them. Most will become lapsed users of the program as they generally fail to accumulate sufficient points to qualify for rewards and so gradually forget about, or reject, the program (e.g. they lose the loyalty card). Hopefully a few of these consumers will become heavier buyers.[6]

---

5   Chapter 4 shows the skewed pattern of buying rates (negative binomial distribution). The rate of category buying is also typically very skewed with lighter than average buyers being the norm (this follows a gamma distribution).

6   Some consumers will become heavier buyers because of the law of buyer moderation, not because the loyalty program changed their behaviour.

If a loyalty program only recruits highly loyal buyers (right-hand quadrants) it has little chance of generating any change; first, these people don't need to change their behaviour to win rewards, and second, they can't change anyway as they are already very loyal. It is because of these consumers that a loyalty program can have negative effects: it gives away rewards but gains no change in behaviour in return.

Consumers that fall into the lower left-hand are the most desirable consumers for a loyalty program to recruit. If a loyalty program reaches consumers who are heavy buyers of a category and who are not 100% loyal to a brand, then it is more likely to extract additional loyalty and sales. These heavy buyers have more loyalty to give; however, their motivation is not necessarily high as they will earn rewards anyway. What motivation they have is also easily countered by competitor loyalty programs and promotions. These heavy buyers are very aware of competitor offerings.

With this knowledge of the structure of the market, and the nature of loyalty programs, logic suggests that such programs have little chance of generating increased sales and profit. A loyalty program's success depends on recruiting many consumers from the lower left-hand quadrant, which is unlikely. Ideally, from a cost perspective, a program needs to recruit as few consumers as possible who are already loyal to the brand (this, however, is probably impossible). What happens in the real world? As you have probably suspected, loyalty programs are good at recruiting existing buyers of a brand (both heavy and light category buyers) but lousy at recruiting heavy category buyers who are not current buyers of a brand.

Table 11.3 shows the category buying rate of members and non-members of a loyalty program.[7] The table clearly shows that loyalty programs fail to attract a disproportionate number of heavier buyers.

---

7   The data in Table 11.3 comes from our original loyalty program panel data in Australia, plus a replication study in New Zealand. This particular analysis had not been previously reported.

Table 11.3: Buying rates of members and non-members of a loyalty program

Category	Average purchase frequency	
	Consumers who joined the program	Consumers who did not join the program
Supermarkets	27	28
Retail fuel	13	14
Department stores	10	9
Credit cards	10	9
Telecommunications	26	26
Petrol	12	13
Credit cards	9	9
Average	**15**	**15**

Source: Ehrenberg-Bass Institute.

In spite of the discussion above, this discovery is a little surprising because heavier category buyers (both regular buyers of a brand and non-buyers) have much more to gain from a loyalty program. It makes sense to expect that loyalty program members would be heavier buyers (of a category).

What this shows is that mental and physical availability is the dominant driver of recruitment to loyalty programs—ahead of the attractiveness of the rewards. Existing buyers of a brand join, i.e. both heavy and light buyers of the category. This suggests that the best way to promote a loyalty program, and recruit members, is to avoid using a brand's own stores, website or mailing list. Ideally, a brand would recruit members in its competitors' stores! Unfortunately, it is extremely difficult to overcome the inherent characteristics of a loyalty program—that it will skew towards existing buyers of the brand. This is why loyalty programs can't have much effect. They essentially reward existing buyers for what they already do.

Loyalty programs are not good at affecting loyalty. They are more suited to being used to build a database of consumers, creating a new channel to talk to consumers and a way of monitoring their buying in-store.

This is a very expensive and difficult endeavour, and has more value to some marketers than others.[8] Most loyalty programs need to collect or utilise this data if they are to recoup their investment.

Conclusion

This chapter has shown that loyalty programs have little effect. It has also revealed that knowledge of scientific laws can lead to insight, prediction and understanding. If all brand managers had known of these laws billions of dollars would not have been spent on poor performing marketing investments like loyalty programs.

---

8   Dunnhumby's work for Tesco and Kroger, among others, stands out for successfully building a useful database based on loyalty program membership.

Mental and Physical Availability

Byron Sharp

The key marketing task is to make a brand easy to buy; this requires building mental and physical availability. Everything else is secondary. Brands largely compete in terms of physical and mental (brand salience) availability. Even product innovation largely works, when it works, through enhancing brand salience and gaining further distribution. Building mental availability requires distinctiveness and clear branding. Building physical availability requires breadth and depth of distribution in space and in time. Together, mental and physical availability make a brand easier to buy for more people, in more situations.

A new theory of competition for sales

We have a collection of scientific laws of marketing—law-like patterns that hold very widely and under known conditions (see the complete list of marketing laws on pages vii–viii). These laws can be used to predict and explain marketing patterns, but it would also be useful to have a theory that could weave these laws into a memorable, overarching story that can guide our marketing strategy.

Table 12.1: The new consumer behaviour model

Past world view	Attitude drives behaviour	Brand loyals	Brand switchers	Deeply committed buyers	Involvement	Rational, involved viewers
New world view	Behaviour largely drives attitude	Loyal switchers	Loyal switchers	Uncaring cognitive misers	Heuristics	Emotional, distracted viewers

Table 12.2: The new brand performance model

Past world view	Growth through targeting brand loyals	Unpredictable, confusing brand metrics	Price promotions win new customers	Target marketing	We compete on positioning	Differentiation
New world view	Growth through penetration	Predictable, meaningful brand metrics	Price promotions reach existing loyal customers	Sophisticated mass marketing	We compete with all brands in the category	Distinctiveness

Table 12.3: The new advertising model

Past world view	Positioning	Message comprehension	Unique selling propositions	Persuasion	Teaching	Campaign bursts
New world view	Salience	Getting noticed, emotional response	Relevant associations	Refreshing and building memory structures	Reaching	Continuous presence

This theory has to be a new replacement for the twentieth century Kotlerian view of marketing. According to Kotler, competition for sales is about creating differentiated brands that carve off sections of market share by addressing the demand for heterogeneity. Thus, competing brands sell to different types of consumers; brands have substantially different images; and brand loyalty varies considerably. This view also holds that many brands are niche brands; and that considerable growth is possible by becoming even more niche and selling more to a brand's most loyal customers.

This worldview was partly responsible for the very large (and low return) investments in loyalty programs and customer relationship management (CRM) that occurred towards the end of the twentieth century.[1] On a less visible level, this worldview was also responsible for millions of misguided and productivity-sapping marketing plans. Some marketers got lucky and succeeded in spite of their plan,[2] through implementation 'mistakes' or from competitors getting it even more wrong. But many misplaced plans did their bit to erode their brand's customer franchise.

However, this twentieth century view of marketing is not completely wrong. It just describes a limited part of the competition for sales. It more aptly describes the competition between product categories than the competition between brands within a category (yet, even in this case it is often an exaggeration). The Kotlerian view doesn't fit the facts of branded competition; it fails the most basic test of scientific theories: it does not lead to laws. In some cases, it directly counters these laws (i.e. it predicts different patterns). For example, strong differentiation and differences in brand user profiles would destroy the laws of double jeopardy and duplication of purchase. Yet in the real world we find only minor deviations from these laws. The Kotlerian worldview is not the opposite of reality, but it

---

1   Philip Kotler was among the many consultants advocating such investments. He said marketing practice had previously focused too much on acquiring customers and not enough on trying to improve customer retention (Kotler, 1992).

2   Some patients of medieval blood-letting doctors survived and returned to health in spite of their doctoring.

is a very poor representation of it. It's similar to the view that the world is flat—it isn't, though there are flattish parts (Australia, for instance).

To understand the new theory of branded competition for sales we need to consider the hectic complicated world of real consumers.

Busy buyers

As discussed in Chapter 4, most customers are very light, occasional buyers of a brand. A brand is a very small part of its customers' lives; people don't think much about brands, even the ones they buy—after all there are so many brands. This is largely why brands advertise, to ensure that customers don't forget to buy them.

Yet it is difficult to talk to buyers because they are so busy with their lives. Machines used to be referred to as 'labour-saving devices' because it was thought that they would lead to more leisure time. Instead, new technology has squeezed even more into our already busy lives. For example, the global impact of the mobile phone has been dramatic. We used to spend a lot of time waiting for other people. Now, meetings can be replaced with an immediate phone call; waiting for others to arrive is replaced by a call or text message to see where they are; agendas and locations can be changed in minutes. Time is precious, we all only have one life, and it is a human trait to try to do more with the time we have.

For marketers, this makes the task of getting attention very difficult. On top of this, when people aren't working they have many more interesting things to think about than brands! I'm not just referring to the really important things in life like family, friends, politics, hobbies, sport and saving the planet. Yahoo US reported that the top search terms for 2008 were:

1	Britney Spears	**6**	Jessica Alba
2	WWE (world wrestling entertainment)	**7**	Naruto
3	Barack Obama	**8**	Lindsay Lohan
4	Miley Cyrus	**9**	Angelina Jolie
5	RuneScape	**10**	American Idol

This is what people really think about! Also, six out of the top ten were the same as the previous year. Over the past decade, Britney Spears has been an incredibly popular search term; she has been the most popular for seven out of the past eight years. Google no longer releases lists of the top Google search terms, but you can bet that Britney is at the top. (Part of Google's genius was the early work they did to identify all the potential misspellings of things so that Google users found what they were looking for.[3]) No wonder brands employ celebrities and try to piggy-back their ability to get attention.

A cluttered world

One of the things we are cramming into our lives is more commercial media, and hence more advertising. There are plenty of uninformed reports of massive declines in television viewing, but this just isn't happening. In general, people are not replacing television viewing with web browsing—they have simply added the internet to all the other media they consume. People are also consuming more media than ever before. In 2005, Ball State University's Centre for Media Design undertook a large observational study of US consumers and found that (commercial and non-commercial) media consumption (listening, viewing and reading) covered about 30% of people's waking day, with television still, by far, the most dominant media in terms of both penetration and hours of exposure (in line with the double jeopardy law).

A typical viewer of television—who watches only an hour and a half of television a day[4]—is exposed to more than 60 ads. If a typical viewer also

---

3   This web page <www.google.com/jobs/britney.html> provides real examples of the many misspellings of Britney Spears' name that Google's spelling correction system has been developed to deal with.

4   The typical television viewer watches less television than the average viewer (i.e. most of us watch less than the average). This is because television viewing, like brand buying, is skewed: there are a few very heavy viewers (who watch almost everything) and many light viewers.

reads one magazine or newspaper he or she will be exposed to anywhere from a few dozen to a few hundred more ads. Radio and the internet are also cluttered with advertising, and then there is the general background of advertising seen while walking the streets.[5] Therefore, realistically, a person may be exposed to a few hundred advertising messages per day. This is far lower than the level of exposure disseminated by popular mythology, but this level of realistic exposure is still high considering that people don't live to consume advertising. Attentively consuming all these ads would take three hours out of a person's waking day!

So each ad has to fight for a tiny piece of attention. How many ads can you recall that you saw or heard this morning? Much advertising receives no active attention whatsoever, or not enough for the receiver to take in which brand is being advertised. Remember the television study mentioned in Chapter 1: a mere 16% of viewers noticed a particular commercial and correctly named the advertised brand.

How consumers cope

The typical supermarket stocks around 30 000 products (brands and their variants). It seems incredible that consumers can enter a supermarket and leave with their shopping before closing time. How do they find and select brands? Consumers adopt a number of useful strategies. A very important strategy is that we 'satisfice'[6] rather than optimise. Rather than working hard to find the best product for us, we settle for something that we consider good or satisfactory. Some economists rightly point out

---

5   The first Nielsen GPS survey estimated that the average American was (potentially) exposed to 40 outdoor ads a day (*MediaWeek*, 7 December 2005). Again, this will be a skewed average, with the typical consumer being exposed to fewer than 40 ads per day.

6   This term was coined by Nobel Prize-winning economist Herbert A Simon (1957). It is a portmanteau of the two words: satisfaction and suffice.

that such behaviour is optimal, considering the full cost of gaining the necessary information to make a better buy.[7]

Brand loyalty is a natural behaviour that is based on this satisficing strategy. For many different reasons—many of which could be called 'habit' or 'convenience'—we buy the same few brands over and over again and simplify buying decisions by only noticing our few regular brands. Often we don't want to make choices; we are pressed for time, or tired, or really just don't care. We seldom ever want a large selection from which to choose as it's too difficult. So we restrict our consideration set down to a few favoured brands.

Marketing theory pays insufficient attention to this coping behaviour. Instead, theories about buyer behaviour are obsessed with brand evaluation. Obsession is a strong word, and yet it is justified because marketing texts instruct their readers to deliver products and services that fulfil customer needs better than other brands; consultants advise brand managers to make buyers emotionally committed to their brand; and market research (from choice modelling to focus groups) is largely concerned with whether or not customers think a brand's features are the best.

Yet the most important part of any buyer's purchasing process (i.e. the part that marketers should be the most interested in) occurs almost entirely without being noticed. This part of the process occurs before buyers consciously evaluate which brand to choose: *buyers, in effect, 'decide' not to consider the vast majority of brands on the market.* Instead they notice a few and quite often, only one.

Most brands are effectively ignored, and sometimes no evaluation between brands takes place; for example, if we want a mortgage, we get one from our bank; if we want legal advice, we ring our lawyer; if we want

---

7   In cybernetics the (technical) term 'satisfice' means a computer decision-making program that explicitly factors in the cost of making a decision. After the 1997 chess game where IBM's 'Deep Blue' beat chess master Garry Kasparov, he remarked that the computer was 'playing like a human' after it adopted a satisficing position. Kasparov said that a successful strategy in beating computers was to predict the most rational move, but when computers starting adopting satisficing positions these predictions failed.

toothpaste, we look for our preferred brand on the shelf. This lack of evaluation and consideration of alternatives can occur even when a consumer is standing in front of a supermarket shelf that is filled with choices.

Screening out is a natural behaviour, people do it all the time; for example, screening out other people talking in the room,[8] screening out advice from parents, etc. Buyers don't care that there are many brands they do not consider, because the ones they do consider perform well enough. However, it matters enormously to marketers—their brands need to be noticed and considered. Being noticed and considered is often the biggest factor in why a brand is bought or not. Given how small buyers' consideration sets are, a brand has more than a 'sporting chance' of being bought if it is noticed and considered. So, a brand's sales are primarily determined by how many consideration sets it failed to enter.

Similarly, in dealing with the vast volume of marketing communication people adopt incredibly capable filtering mechanisms that mean they don't have to process most advertising. That's why we can watch an ad over and over and still get the brand name wrong.

Evaluation is less important than we think

We don't notice ourselves not noticing things—it's a subconscious process. This is perhaps why marketers and academics largely ignore this aspect of buyer behaviour. Both academic and commercial marketing researchers work from an evaluation-centred view of buyer behaviour. Billions of dollars are spent on researching brand features and perceptions because these are considered to be the dominant reasons why customers buy or not. This belief is undermined by the following facts:

1 What buyers remember about brands (and which brands they remember) varies across buying occasions. Memories are

---

8   Yet we have an amazing ability to hear when someone, on the other side of a busy room, mentions our name. Clearly screening out does include some unconscious processing of stimuli. This gives us some clues about how to get around the screening out mechanism.

imperfect and variable, as buyers are busy and have limited time to devote to any single purchase (or single market research question).

2 A buyer only considers a tiny subset of the brands they know; they do not evaluate most of the different feature-bundles on the market. Consumers typically know a little bit about some brands and almost nothing about most brands. Customers rarely think about (the features of) these less familiar brands, let alone buy them.

3 Which brand a buyer purchases (from the one or few brands they happened to consider on the day) depends on a myriad of factors that relate to the situation and circumstances. Sometimes a buyer is feeling extravagant, frugal, patriotic, etc. Evaluation criteria can, and do, change 'on the fly'. So any actual evaluation that occurs can vary wildly each time a customer goes to buy.

Evaluation is therefore less important and less predictable than our market research techniques assume.

So why are some brands much more popular than others? Why, in the US, are many more Fords sold than Renaults? A part of the answer might be that when buyers actively consider both Ford and Renault they prefer Ford—perhaps Ford is better? Yet this is odd because in some markets, like France, Renault outsells Ford. Also, Renault owners throughout the world report similar satisfaction to Ford owners. The main answer to the question is that many more car buyers remember to consider Ford than Renault. In most markets Renault seldom gets a look in. This is not because people dislike Renault or think that it lacks desirable features. It is just that, outside of France, few people think of Renault.[9]

---

9   Several of my friends have noted that when visiting Adelaide, Australia, they often purchase and drink iced coffee; yet rarely, if ever, do so when they are in their home countries, even though they could. Being in Adelaide reminds them they like iced coffee, but they forget this the moment they get home. This isn't because Adelaide has much better iced coffee, nor because Adelaide has abundant sunshine, but rather because it is a very popular and prominent drink in Adelaide. There are well-advertised commercial brands that are stocked in every store (sales exceed Coca-Cola), and every cafe prominently offers its own iced coffee. Similarly, I find myself eating burgers whenever I'm in the US.

So the big marketing issue is how to get a brand thought of, more often, in more buying situations; in other words, how to build mental availability.

In any market, many more people buy one brand over another or an individual buys one brand more than he or she buys all the others. This phenomenon typically leads to the intuitive, but largely incorrect, conclusion that there must be perceived difference between brands. But differences in perceived product features (or brand image/positioning) only marginally explain why one brand is chosen more or less than another. It is screening out behaviour (and physical availability) that largely explains the vast and continuing market share differences that exist between even highly similar brands.

This suggests a simple prescription: get people to think of a brand. Yet there is nothing simple about this. One of the hardest ongoing battles any marketer faces is to get light, occasional and non-customers to think of their brand. Buyers have too many other more interesting (non-marketing) things to think about. Even brands with plenty of customers still have to fight for customers' attention. Buyers have so many other things going on in their lives that each category (let alone brand) purchase is trivial. What a battle it is for all the vast number of brands in the market to strive for snippets of attention.[10] This gives us a major clue into how brands compete for buying occasions.

How brands really compete

Decades of research into the patterns in buying behaviour and marketing metrics has led to the surprising conclusion that brands compete for custom primarily in terms of mental and physical availability. Brands that are easier to buy, for more people in more occasions, get bought more often. Brands that have greater market share are better known (and more noticed) by more people and are more widely available. In other words,

---

10   And you thought the competitors in a single category were enough!

brands with larger market share have greater physical and mental availability, and also have larger marketing budgets to support these assets.

Surprisingly, other brand differences have little impact. As discussed in Chapter 8, McDonald's, Pizza Hut and KFC are differentiated in many ways, not least in that they sell different food (burgers, pizza and fried chicken respectively), yet they compete as fast food brands (with McDonald's maintaining its advantage of greater mental and physical availability). Each fast food brand sells to the same sorts of buyers (who hold similar attitudes about the brand(s) they use); fast food brands share buyers with each other as if their products are direct substitutes. Indeed, fast food brands spend considerable time reminding buyers of their similarities (e.g. McDonald's stresses that it offers chicken (burgers) and KFC stresses that it offers (chicken) burgers).

Competition in terms of mental and physical availability fits the empirical facts observed in all product categories (see pages vii–viii for a list of marketing laws):

• Brands within a product category sell to nearly identical consumer bases; each brand's consumer base varies from the others chiefly in terms of size (i.e. the number of buyers), not in demographics, psychographics, personality characteristics, values or attitudes (see Chapter 5).

• Buyers of a brand seldom view their brand as being different from its competitors—whether for symbolic, emotional or more prosaic reasons. Buyers very rarely view different brands as being unacceptable. Buyers of different brands express similar attitudes about their brand and similar reasons for buying it. When buyers adopt a new brand their attitudes change in favour of that brand. Buyers simply know and like the brands they buy, and they are vastly more likely to notice, consider and buy these brands over others. Regardless of a lack of differentiation at a brand level or added values, brands have real market-based assets and loyal buyers.

- Buyers are polygamously loyal; they have personal repertoires of brands that they purchase repeatedly; they are seldom 100% loyal, and are never exclusively loyal in the long term. Therefore, competing brands share consumers; they do so with every other brand in the category, and how much they share depends on the other brand's market share. For example, all soft drink brands share more customers with Coca-Cola than with Fanta. Also, when soft drink brands gain sales, they steal sales from all the other brands in proportion to the market share of the other brands. Partitions of brands that share more or less of their buyers with each other are weak—all brands in a category compete as if they were close substitutes in spite of their physical or perceived differences. Diet Pepsi and Diet Coke do share buyers more than predicted, but both still share far more of their buyers with Coca-Cola and any other brands with a large market share.

These empirical patterns show that brands largely compete as branded versions of the product category, with their function, image and price differentiation (within limits) being of surprisingly low importance.

Mental availability

Mental availability/brand salience is the propensity for a brand to be noticed and/or thought of in buying situations.[11] The term brand salience is sometimes used synonymously with top-of-mind brand awareness measures (e.g. the first financial institution recalled when asked, 'Which financial institutions can you name?'). However, the term brand salience means more than that. There is a real problem with all brand-awareness measures that assume the link to the name of the product category is all that needs to be measured.

---

11   This 'mental availability' section is based on an Ehrenberg-Bass Institute report: Romaniuk and Sharp 2004a.

Mental availability is based on the network structure in buyers' memories. For example, memory associations for a bank brand include:

- a branch near work
- home loans
- internet banking
- friends bank there
- a branch on high street
- someone I know worked there
- can get cash out
- Visa
- my first credit card (and the bike I bought)
- the colour, logo, staff uniform, etc.

A simple explanation about how memory works is that memory consists of 'nodes' that hold pieces of information. If two pieces of information are associated (e.g. Coca-Cola and red), links exist between these nodes. Buyers have a network of information (also referred to as brand associations) linked to a brand name. For example, McDonald's is associated with hamburgers, yellow arches and fast food. These links are developed and refreshed through experiences such as buying and using the brand, being exposed to marketing activities (such as advertising) and hearing about other people's experiences.

There are other aspects of memory, such as sensory memory for smell and taste, and the retrieval of emotions such as joy and pain, but they are more often recalled after a brand is thought of. For example, you think of McDonald's and you have fond memories of your child's last birthday (or not!); whereas for brand salience we are primarily interested in what makes McDonald's thought of and/or noticed.

The more extensive and fresher the network of memory associations about a brand, the greater the brand's chance of being noticed or thought of in the variety of buying situations experienced by customers.

Such memory associations also increase the chance of a brand being selected when multiple options are present.

Therefore, building mental availability is about developing different memory links (that relate to a brand) to increase the scope of the brand-related network in people's memories—the brand's share of mind.

More than awareness

Traditional awareness concepts of recognition and recall are typically driven by their measures,[12] which are invariably single cue measures (i.e. almost always the product category for recall, 'What brands of power tools are you aware of?') or the brand name for recognition ('Have you heard of the brand "Black & Decker"?'). Variations on this theme, like top-of-mind awareness or speed of recall, don't depart from this practice of using only a single cue. Not surprisingly, these measures crudely capture individuals' memory structures and poorly predict the frequency that a brand will be noticed or recalled in buying situations. These measures are akin to trying to estimate how often a coin will land on 'heads' by tossing it only once.

Brand salience depends on a brand's share of people's minds, by which I mean the quantity and quality of memory links to and from a brand. Quantity refers to the number of associations a buyer has about a brand name. Quality has two aspects: strength of association and relevance of the attribute. First, some memory links are stronger than others, in that they are more likely to be activated. For example, for some people, the cue 'Elvis Presley' may always bring fried peanut butter sandwiches to mind and vice versa.[13] For these people, this is a strong association— yet for many others this may be a very occasional association. Second, some memory links are more relevant to buying situations than others.

---

12 In turn, these measures are driven by the practicalities of market research. One reason that brand awareness is synonymous with the brand name cue is that telephone interviewing dominated the last 20 to 30 years of market research. Showing the brand, or its distinctive assets, was difficult over the telephone.

13 Fried peanut butter sandwiches were one of Elvis Presley's favourite foods.

Elvis Presley is unlikely to be a cue that people encounter when they are in a position to buy peanut butter. However, this association is not entirely unimportant, as hearing an Elvis song increases the chance of people thinking about peanut butter, and by doing so, enhancing links to cues that do occur during buying situations.

When a brand scores well on traditional awareness measures but its sales are disappointing, the common conclusion is that buyers don't like the brand. However, the problem can be that, while buyers know of the brand (and find it acceptable), they seldom think of it or notice it when they are in buying situations.

Buyers use different cues when retrieving brands as buying options. For example, cues for something to eat in the morning may include something low in fat, something healthy and something quick. Buyers may also use more abstract cues—like colour and the style or size of the packaging—to identify and notice specific brands. They may be totally unaware of the cues they are utilising.

By building memory links to attributes marketers can increase:

a   the number of people who think of a particular brand
b   the number of times each person thinks of a particular brand as an option (to buy).

Linking a brand to attributes means the brand now has some probability to be bought; this is an infinitely higher chance of being bought than when the brand was not thought of at all.

No consumer is wedded to one attribute all the time. This is a common mistake made in segmentation research. For example, rarely is someone always interested in buying something healthy in a product category (or in life!). The typical buyer might be thinking healthy one time, convenient next time and a treat the time after. Buyers use different attributes at different points in time. Context can matter a lot; for example, ice-creams are more likely to be recalled as a food or treat option at the beach and during holidays. Buyers can also use multiple attributes on a single occasion (e.g. convenient and a treat). The attributes can come from anything relevant to the buying context. So it is necessary for marketers to have a broad understanding of the thought processes that consumers go through before they even think of any brands as options to buy. Researching this isn't just a matter of asking consumers, because much of this memory functioning is unconscious.

Cue competitors

Different cues also mean that different competitors are likely to be thought of as options by the buyer at any one time. Competitive options don't even have to be in the same product category. For example, 'something to wake me up' can conjure a coffee, a Coca-Cola, a Pepsi, a brisk walk or a swim. When marketers think of competitors they often think of functional look-alikes. However, it is better to think of competitors as 'cue competitors'. Competitors are all other options linked to the cue, as these are most likely to be thought of and compete for selection.

The importance of distinctive brand assets

Over time brands build memory structures; most of these are very simple, such as associations with colour, pack shape, fonts and tone. These associations are vital because they allow consumers to recognise a brand and its advertising. In other words, associations allow a brand's communications to do their job of refreshing salience and building new memory structures. Without these distinctive brand assets it is difficult for consumers to digest a brand's communications. Failure to employ these distinctive elements in communication can also mean that existing customers screen out the communication as they do for the brands that they don't use.

So the maintenance of brand salience depends on the quality of branding and advertising. Distinctive, consistent icons and imagery build memory associations that allow a brand to be noticed and recalled in a range of buying situations. This is a huge part of brand custodianship, yet it is often overlooked; marketers often fail to deploy a brand's distinctive assets and, in effect, they sabotage them.

Physical availability

Physical availability means making a brand as easy to notice and buy as possible, for as many consumers as possible, across as wide a range of potential buying situations as possible. This includes more than retail penetration, but also presence in store. It includes hours of availability, and ease of facilitating the purchase. Being easy to notice and buy is essential, because buyers do not have strong preferences even for the brands they are loyal to; they are happy to buy alternatives from within their personal repertoires (and they regularly do).

I'm surprised how often marketers of consumer goods and services will say, 'Oh well, we have practically 100% availability'. They point to their brand's presence in all the leading supermarket chains, or their national branch network or their web site that can take orders 24 hours a day. None of this comes close to 100% availability. Perhaps the problem is the word 'availability'; I don't mean 'available if a consumer is motivated to seek out the product', I mean readily available. Like the often reported desire of Coca-Cola to be no more than an 'arm's length' away. Against a standard like this, it's easy to see that every marketer has potential to improve the physical availability of its brand.

How brands compete for sales

In the long run, brands essentially compete in terms of mental and physical availability. Even product innovation largely works (when it works) by enhancing brand salience and gaining further physical distribution. Building brand salience requires distinctiveness and clear branding, but brands seldom compete on meaningful differentiation. This means that marketing attention should be focused on building these assets so that a brand is easier to buy, for more people and in more buying situations.

Long-run profits

One of the things that makes established brands so valuable is that mental and physical availability takes a long time to build and a long time to fade.

This stability is worth money. Brands, whether large or small, are able to survive, often for very long periods, because they are able to maintain their market-based assets of mental and physical availability. Growth depends on enhancing these assets. Even temporary advantages (such as advances in products or services) can enhance these potentially sustainable assets. Advantages that do not enhance these assets have no long-term value. For example, price promotions, because of their lack of reach, do little or nothing to enhance mental and physical ability, even though such promotions cause increases in sales. When the price promotion ends, everything returns to normal largely because price promotions reach so few buyers, and are particularly poor at reaching new buyers.[14]

Mental and physical availability—a brand's market-based assets

Over the past twenty years there has been growing appreciation for the intangible assets that underpin the financial value of corporations (Sharp 1995; Srivastava, Shervani & Fahey, 1998). These assets can be sold, and they are generally worth far more than a corporation's tangible assets. Mental and physical availability, and the brand's distinctive iconography (discussed in Chapter 8) are assets that can be sold. They are brand equity.

These are *market-based* assets, in that they come about through trading activity. They are created by marketing. They are assets because they cost money to build, and other companies may purchase them rather than spending the money and time (and taking the risk) to build their own. They are valuable because they provide some surety of future profit.

These market-based assets deliver productivity. Advertising works better when there are existing memory structures in viewers' heads—so

---

14 In Chapter 10 John Scriven also speculates that price promotions fail to have long-term effects because they don't build or refresh memory structures. This is surprising (purchasing and consumption should help memory structures), but there is growing evidence that points to the difference between advertising and price promotions. This is discussed and explained in Chapter 9 on advertising.

long as the advertising works with these memory structures. Advertising also works better when the brand has plenty of physical availability. Advertising falls on barren ground when it reaches consumers who aren't near a brand's sales points.

To marketers, these market-based assets provide security—next year's sales will be not too dissimilar to this year's. This is very valuable, though it also creates problems in evaluating marketing actions. Every action is moderated by these assets, so marketplace reactions become sluggish. We see this in price elasticities where larger brands have lower elasticities (see Chapter 10); it's the same for other marketing stimulus like advertising; it's harder to see anything happening when you turn it on and off.

To clearly see or statistically model the effects of a marketing strategy, look at a small brand with little mental and physical availability. In particular, this will show a nice, neat sales reaction to increasing distribution—a near perfect correlation: double your distribution and sales will double. Measuring marketing is less simple for established brands.[15]

When marketing support has been absent for a long time for a brand that retains considerable market-based assets, tremendous gains can be made by sprucing up the marketing mix—particularly brand salience in the minds of consumers and retailers. This is one way to make your fortune: find a brand that was popular, with substantial mental and physical availability, but that has been neglected and so has lost much market share. Fix the product quality, lower the price, start advertising again, and if necessary, work to regain breadth and depth of distribution.

---

15   This phenomenon appears in the work of Berk Ataman and Professors Mela and van Heerde to model the relative effects marketing mix elements over time. In their examination of many extremely small new grocery brand launches, their statistical modelling finds the effects of distribution gains (in supermarkets) are dominant. However, when they analysed established brands, advertising spend levels turned out to be more important. This highlights a difficulty that marketing mix modelling faces in comparing effects across brands. Each has different market-based assets, which moderate the sales effects of the marketing mix. And new brands have quite different market-based assets than established ones.

McDonald's is a good example of this. As the twenty-first century began, McDonald's growth in developed countries slowed and it was being regularly criticised for selling unhealthy food. As companies like Subway and Starbucks rolled out stores across the world, it looked like McDonald's marketers were 'asleep at the wheel'. In hindsight, it was a terrible blunder to have missed the trend towards drinking real coffee, which hit America fast as it started to catch up with the rest of the developed world. McDonald's eventually looked outside its stores and saw that people were eating and drinking (a little) better. So they introduced 'innovations' like salads, sandwiches, soft chairs and the McCafe, which served proper coffee. The sales results were superb; McDonald's bounced back. Nothing McDonald's did was innovative; it was completely a 'me too' catch-up exercise, the sort of thing that is frowned upon by marketing texts. My favourite McDonald's 'innovation' in Australia was the introduction of a toasted cheese and tomato sandwich. This is something that is available at nearly every deli and cafe in the country. McDonald's didn't do anything radical; it just got competitive again. But thanks to its existing mental and physical availability it can sell a lot of coffee and toasted sandwiches.

Essentially, McDonald's took away a 'reason not to buy', which was undermining its market-based assets. Remember, much of the marketing battle is to get into the usually very small consideration set; when this happens, which is far less often than any marketer would like, the last thing you want to be is rejected for some reason (e.g. it contains trans fat, is too expensive, too salty, the store is too far, Sarah won't like it).

A classic example of exploiting neglected, market-based assets occurred near my office in the 1990s. A large wine company, Seppelt, purchased a small, old, run-down Barossa Valley winery by the name of 'Queen Adelaide'. The Queen Adelaide winery had begun in 1858; its wines had once been popular, but were now mostly seen in dusty bargain bins. The Seppelt winemakers took this brand and combined their modern, quality wine (nothing flash or expensive but clean with clear fruit) with the Queen Adelaide label. Almost overnight, Queen Adelaide became the largest-selling chardonnay in Australia. I don't think the old Queen Adelaide even had a chardonnay in its range, but chardonnay was now popular and Queen Adelaide was still a very well-known brand. A decent marketing mix and already established market-based assets re-created a big-selling brand very quickly. This gave Seppelt a fabulous financial return on its purchase of a run-down, old winery.

The Ehrenberg-Bass Institute recently analysed submissions for the advertising effectiveness awards in Australia (similar to the Effies in the US).[16] It's well known that such awards tend to attract new product campaigns, because it's easier for them to show the effects of their advertising when they start from sales of zero (and the advertising gets the credit for the success of the new product). Similarly, we found that more than half the submissions from established brands were cases of advertising being started again after a very long hiatus.

For marketers of established brands, everything they do is moderated by the brand's market-based assets. Their job is not so much to stimulate current sales but to maintain and build the brand's market-based assets. Such marketers should be less concerned with producing sales blips with short-lived campaigns, and much more concerned with building mental and physical availability.

Thomas Bayne, CEO of Mountain View Learning, suggests marketers should adopt a balance sheet-style document to assess their marketing efforts. The balance sheet lists what is most likely to reinforce or build mental and physical availability and what is least likely. Table 12.4 is an example of such a document (to which you might like to add). Remember, any marketing activity that skews to part of the customer base (particularly to the heavier, more loyal customers) is unlikely to build mental or physical availability.

---

16 See <www.effie.org>. The advertising for the American launch of Nintendo's Wii won an Effie in 2008.

Table 12.4 Marketing 'balance sheet'

Very likely to reinforce or build mental and physical availability	Unlikely to reinforce or build mental and physical availability	Unknown or highly risky
Broadening distribution	Coupons and price promotions	Advertising that contains new information
Gaining a new distribution channel	Packaging changes	Competitions
Consistent use of a brand's distinctive assets	Loyalty programs	Temporary (e.g. limited edition) product variants
Consistent advertising		Comparative advertising
Broad-reaching media		Suspense advertising (i.e. the brand name is hidden)
Gaining shelf space in another area of a store		
Broad range of product varieties and pack formats and sizes		

Seven simple rules for marketing

The purpose of science is to simplify the enormously complex world we live in; to allow us to glimpse some of its regularities; to give us the power of prediction; and to provide insight into why things are the way they are.

The marketing world is extraordinarily complex, but textbooks fail us when they suggest that this complexity can never be mastered. As we've seen, there *are* regularities in buying behaviour and sales performance. So it is possible to come up with some simple rules for 'branded competition for sales' (i.e. competition to build a sales base with considerable lasting capability). This is, almost without exception, competition between brands[17] (entities whose sales are underpinned by *both* mental and physical availability).

---

17 I'm indebted to Professor Guenther Mueller-Heumann for pointing out to me that (aside from a few mining companies) all major corporations are built on brands.

Within this area there are strategic guidelines:

1 Continuously reach all buyers of the brand's service/product category, with both physical distribution and marketing communication.
2 Ensure the brand is easy to buy.
3 Get noticed. Without some processing, the brand's communication dollars are wasted.
4 Refresh and build brand-linked memory structures that make the brand easier to notice and buy.
5 Create distinctive communication assets.
6 Be consistent, yet fresh and interesting.
7 Stay competitive, keep up the mass appeal; don't give customers reasons not to buy the brand.

Rule 1: Reach

Reach all consumers of the brand's service/product category, both with physical distribution and marketing communication. All these people are potential buyers of the brand. Examine marketing options in terms of their ability to cost effectively reach as many customers as possible. Avoid strategies that fail to reach non-buyers or light buyers of the brand. Most of the brand's sales potential lies with these customers. Reach across geographical space, time and situations. Avoid going 'off air'. Avoid narrow descriptions of the brand's target market that are out of sync with who really buys the brand. Understand who buys, when, and how the brand fits into their lives. Stop talking about your average buyer—there is a wide variety of consumers.

Rule 2: Be easy to buy

Physical and mental availability drive market share because they make the brand easier to buy, for more people, in more situations, across time and space. This requires research to appreciate how consumers buy, and how they fit the brand into their lives. You also need to look out for emerging 'reasons not to buy', like missing pack types or sizes, or prices that are too high.

It's often flippantly stated that the reason for a particular brand's high market share is 'convenience'. This is a shallow explanation; it requires considerable research to work out what convenience is for one product category compared with another. For example, it's been said that Wal-Mart was initially laughed at in the early 1980s when it built large stores outside of city centres. Some said this was too inconvenient, without appreciating the American trend (of the time) of shopping by car and the convenience of having a large range of merchandise in one location. Similarly, Laura and Al Ries predicted the early demise of the iPhone (after a short period where Apple would 'sell quite a few iPhones ... to early adopters and elites'). They said it would fail because the convenience of an all-in-one device was over-rated.[18] In 2007 Apple surprised the world by selling one million iPhones in the first 74 days of its release. A year later, the second generation iPhone sold one million units in just two days: the weekend of its launch.

Marketing 'gurus', it seems, often completely misjudge what is and is not convenient and important to consumers. I recommend relying on empirical market research to understand what can make the brand easy to buy.

Rule 3: Get noticed

Reaching consumers with advertising and physical distribution amounts to little if the brand is not noticed. Brands that are not seen on the shelf (or not seen when gazing down the street or driving past a store) cannot be bought. Advertisements that are not noticed cannot affect memory structures.

Consumers regularly actively avoid advertising. They use new technologies to do so, as well as old techniques like leaving the room during the television commercial break or flicking past the full-page ad. But even more importantly, consumers don't pay much attention to the advertising they are exposed to.

---

18   See <http://ries.typepad.com/ries_blog/2007/03/convergence_fin.html>.

Little attention is not the same as not processing. We notice more than just the things we actively attend to. Otherwise how on earth could we be ever be prompted (e.g. distracted) to shift our attention? Our 'supervisory attentioning system' (du Plessis, 2005) adjusts our focus from one thing to another, but to do this our brain is processing more than just the object of our current attention.

Robert Heath (2001) has written a book on the fact that advertising can affect memory structures even if it is given very little attention. This is true, but it is still better to gain some attention. Heath argues quite well (although from limited data) that emotionally oriented advertising, in particular, can work with low attention processing. Heath is on solid ground when he uses this to argue that measures of advertising recall are poor measures of advertising effect.

However, Erik du Plessis (2005) points out that one of the primary aims of emotional content in advertising is to gain attention. He draws on considerable empirical evidence showing the link between ad liking and ad awareness. Some years prior to meeting Erik, Dr Rachel Kennedy and I had been making the same argument: that the gentle, if complex, emotional reaction of *liking* increased the sales effectiveness of advertising because it encouraged consumers to pay a little more attention. In her doctoral work Rachel showed that, in general, ads that were better liked were also more likely to be correctly branded. She replicated Erik's COMMAP as a model to explain ad liking (see Figure 12.1).

We also know that brand usage has a powerful affect on ad liking and noticing. This fits with the psychological concept of cognitive dissonance; it also fits with the salience concept that we are better able to process things if they relate to established memory structures (see Rule 4 below); and it fits with extensive research showing that we have implicit and explicit memory. Explicit memories are the memories we are able to retrieve into our consciousness, like remembering that yesterday we went to the beach. Implicit memories can't be recalled like this, but evidence of their existence shows up implicitly, such as in test performance. For example, people who are exposed to a statement, even if they can't remember it,

Figure 12.1: A model to explain ad liking

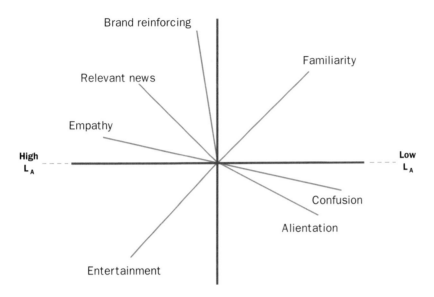

are more likely to rate that statement as true than people not previously exposed to the statement. Another example of this is that respondents are more likely to recall orange coloured brands the day before Halloween (when there were many orange pumpkin lanterns in shop windows). This is known as a priming effect, and it reveals the existence of implicit memory (see Berger & Fitzsimons, 2008). It also shows how we favour the familiar and shows how memory affects our behaviour even when we don't realise it. Even consumers standing in front of supermarket shelves where all the brands are clearly displayed are being powerfully affected by memories—which brands they actually see is affected by memories. This means we may notice a brand on the shelf, and feel slightly more positive about it, simply because we have seen it more (or its advertising more) without the slightest realisation that this has happened.

A well-documented psychological phenomenon is that consumers know how often they have been exposed to a brand (i.e. how often they have seen it advertised or seen it in real life). It seems we have an in-built counting mechanism (see Hasher & Zacks, 1984). As humans evolved this mechanism was presumably very useful in helping to distinguish between the familiar and unfamiliar and to detect subtle differences (e.g. not as many birds in the forest) that might indicate danger.

All this means that clever, likable creativity is a way to get advertising noticed. But it is only one way. What we see depends on what is already in our heads; therefore, the following rules matter too.

Rule 4: Refresh and build memory structures

Even if a brand's advertising is noticed it can't work unless it refreshes or creates useful memory structures for the brand. This requires understanding what consumers already have in their minds and then working with this, not against it. This is the purpose of brand image research, to understand existing memory structures so that communication can be crafted to reflect them.

It's a shame when high-quality, creative advertising fails to do anything for the brand; and yet this happens regularly because the advertising didn't reinforce or build *appropriate* memory structures. For example, Miller Lite ran a wonderful series of 'man law' television commercials. These commercials featured an interesting collection of minor celebrities (like Burt Reynolds) who would debate an issue and make a ruling (a 'man law'). These celebrities ruled on issues like, 'Is the high five overused?', 'If a girl breaks up with your best friend how long do you have to wait before you can ask her out on a date?' and 'Are wireless headsets useful or a technology gone bad?' The advertising campaign attracted much attention: there were web site discussions about man laws, the commercials were posted to YouTube by fans and radio stations mimicked the campaign and held talk-back discussions on their own man laws. However, the commercials didn't look like Miller Lite advertising (the humour was more typical of rival brand, Bud), they said little (if anything) about beer and nothing about Miller. What memory structures did they refresh or build? They built the concept of 'man laws' and tellingly, nearly every YouTube post described the commercials as the 'man law' commercials not the 'Miller Lite' commercials. After months of continued decline in sales, Miller dropped the campaign; as *Advertising Age* wittily stated, Miller decided that market share losses violated man law (Mullman, 2007).

For new brands, the emphasis must be on building the memories that consumers need to buy the brand; for example, what the brand actually does, what it looks like, what the brand name is, where it is sold and where and when it is consumed. These are simple, but essential. Forgetting to tell consumers these things is a marketing sin, as is underestimating how difficult this task will be and how long it may take. With this in mind, simplicity is a virtue. Apple's iPod is a wonderful example. This MP3 player launched into an existing market where there was already considerable choice in technological product features. Digital compressed music was new, slightly complicated technology. Apple launched a single model, with a distinctive, attractive design and characteristic white headphones. The headphones and the play button were prominent, taping into existing memory structures and explaining what the product did. The brand name, iPod, was simple and distinctive; it communicated 'new technology' in a friendly, non-technical manner. And everything was reinforced with the verbal explanation 'A thousand songs in your pocket'. Notice that Apple did not mention the term 'MP3 player'—their advertising didn't talk about this new technology at all. The iPod advertising was also extremely consistent, over time and across media. It always employed the same silhouette figures against colourful backgrounds and these figures were always joyfully dancing (while listening to their iPods) and the white headphones were always obvious. Technical details were left to sales people and web sites to explain, where necessary.[19]

For established brands (i.e. for most advertising) the need to refresh is paramount. Even Coca-Cola's marketers have to remind people that it's a refreshing drink, especially when you are hot. Building a new memory

---

19   The iPod's success is equally if not more a story of great marketing rather than just great integrated hardware and software. It's undoubtedly a very good competitive product, and well priced, but commentators forget that when it launched it was a high end and so expensive MP3 player that could only work with Macintosh computers and could only connect to those newer models that had a fire-wire port. This is a recipe for small sales, but Apple progressively moved to broaden the appeal of the product (e.g. releasing iTunes for Windows) to match its highly successful sophisticated mass marketing.

structure for an existing brand is a long-term project. It's not something that should be taken lightly or undertaken often. Each year's marketing plan should not have a new objective for a new memory structure. Each advertising campaign should largely be saying the same thing. Even when it introduces a piece of new information (e.g. 'Now in blue') it should still tell the old story (i.e. work for the brand).

Rule 5: Create and use distinctive brand assets

Branding matters. Successful businesses have been built by simply introducing branding to a category. For example, Subway recognised that sandwiches were popular throughout the world, and yet there were no branded sandwich shops. What an opportunity sitting under all of our noses! Today, people recognise Subway's brand when they look down a street or drive past. This recognition allows Subway to out compete the less visible, unbranded sandwich shops (even though many are offering a superior product).

There are three main reasons why distinctive brand assets (descriptive memories) matter. First, branding allows consumers to be loyal to particular brands and to adopt heuristics like buying 'their brand' or 'the one they noticed'. Without branding, loyalty (which is a natural behaviour) has to be directed to something else—like a price point, a position on the shelf or 'whatever is on special'.

Second, branding lets consumers know which brand the advertising belongs to so that their memory structures are refreshed for the right brand. Without this, advertising cannot refresh memory structures for a brand (in short, it can't work). The effect is powerful, with consumers who are more familiar with a brand far more likely to notice the brand's advertising.

Branding is the creation of distinctive brand assets. Mental associations act like coat-hangers: they allow other memories and associations with a brand to hang or form. iPod's white headphones (earbuds) are a distinctive asset; even by themselves in any ad they say 'iPod'. The Jolly Green Giant, the M&M characters, PG Tips' chimps, the Mercedes Benz 3-pointed star, Nike's swoosh, Mastercard's 'priceless', L'Oreal's 'because you're worth it', and Puma's puma logo all do the same.

Some brands have developed a portfolio of assets that are visual, aural and verbal. Some assets are more flexible than others and are more easily used across different media.

These assets allow a brand's communication to work. A brand's distinctive imagery isn't processed deeply with any great meaning; consumers seldom pause to think about a brand's logo, name, etc.; certainly not the way that ad agency people do. Let me illustrate this with some examples. Hardly anyone has ever thought about why McDonald's, an American burger chain, has a Scottish name. In Australia there is a successful food brand called Sanitarium (a name not far off sanatorium). In France, P&G don't translate the brand Head&Shoulders into Tete et Épaules; it uses the English brand name. Walker's crisps dominate the UK potato snack category, while Walker's shortbread is probably the most famous Scottish shortbread brand, yet no-one ever asks if it is the same company. Few people ask what Kodak means, or what BMW stands for, or what a name like Fannie Mae has to do with financial services.

A brand's distinctive devices and sounds are processed very quickly by viewers; they are primarily used for recognition, to help work out what is going on and to assist people's brains to access and file information. This is why distinctive brand assets work. This is branding.

Third, distinctive brand assets are so important because these descriptive memories facilitate a brand being noticed. We are able to see a brand because we recognise its iconography. Given that even in a retail setting when we are looking for things to buy we still don't notice most things in the store, distinctive brand assets make a brand salient.

Table 12.5: Examples of distinctive assets

McDonald's	The golden arches (yellow on red), sesame seeds on a bun, Ronald McDonald clown
Coca-Cola	The contour bottle, red, the swirl
Disney	The castle, Mickey mouse ears, Tinkerbell, Pixar's animated lamp

Rule 6: Be consistent, yet fresh

The potential longevity of brands is considerable. Compared with the lifespan of companies, or the professional lifespan of managers, brands seem immortal. The brands that have dominated for decades have done so by being consistent, not by repositioning.

Too often this is forgotten, and the desire to present something new wins. Similarly, much advertising trips over itself trying to present persuasive, differentiating messages. Consumers are resistant to new ideas, yet they are very happy to be reminded of things they already believe, particularly if it is done in an entertaining way.

A large part of the art of advertising is telling the same story, over and over, but in new and entertaining ways (e.g. the hero saves the day and the bad guy loses).

The negative binomial distribution (NBD) pattern of buying shown in Chapter 4 is a sobering reminder of why brands need to be consistent. This skewed purchasing pattern is matched by a similar pattern of media consumption and advertising viewing. A few consumers have noticed a band's advertising, while the vast bulk of the brand's consumers hardly ever see any—and when they do, it is a long time between exposures. Even the slightest inconsistency is confusing. Not that consumers are often confused by advertising (in the sense of feeling frustrated)—they rarely engage enough with advertising for this to happen. Confusing advertising simply washes over them; they don't take it in.

Packaging changes are particularly hard on a brand's legion of occasional buyers. This is why there are so many stories of companies changing a pack and experiencing a sudden and dramatic drop in sales.

Rule 7: Stay competitive—don't give a reason not to buy

Evaluation is over-rated. Brands largely compete in terms of mental and physical availability. This doesn't mean that product features, and consumer evaluation, aren't important—just that they operate within this battle for attention.

When people go to buy a brand, a huge part of the selection process (yet a part they hardly notice; they don't even think of it as part of the decision) is the act of not noticing and/or not considering most options. A buyer evaluates and selects a very limited number of brands—the ones that are noticed or recalled, which often can be a single brand. So while positive features and perceptions help a brand to be chosen, they only do so when they are part of the selection set (i.e. after the buyer has culled most of the other brands). Over time, feature advantages can build salience; with time they assist in gaining mental and physical availability. This means that advantages in a product's features, while important, are less crucial than the business press makes out. This is especially true for established brands with significant market-based assets.

Another way of putting this is that brands that are easier to buy for more people get bought more. Which reminds me that reasons *not* to buy can therefore be much more important (to sales) than reasons to buy. Generally, marketers are quite sensitive to 'reasons not to buy', or at least to negative publicity. Yet it is not uncommon for marketers to spend much effort trying to communicate a 'reason to buy' ('value proposition', USP, differentiating factor, etc.) and yet be quite blasé about features that turn consumers away. For example, many food products still contain trans fat when they don't need to. In some countries, this means the product has to carry a small warning (like 'contains hydrogenated vegetable fat')—you'd think this would be enough to catch marketers' attention and concern.

High prices can also be another reason not to buy. Too many brands are over-priced and also over-discounted. It's as if marketers know that the price is too high, so out of guilt they regularly discount the product.[20] A brand should be priced competitively: this doesn't mean cheap and it doesn't mean it needs to be given away on special. A competitive price is enough to attract and retain customers. An excessive premium gives customers a reason not to buy, a reason to stop, think and reject the

---

20 Another mistaken justification is the myth that two prices allow the brand to tap into two price segments.

brand.[21] An excessive price also encourages retailers to launch a private-label competitor. None of this is fixed by occasional discounts.

It's very difficult to get consumers to notice a brand; when marketers succeed in this, consumers reward the brand with a degree of loyalty (largely due to habit and inertia). However, this can be ruined if they suddenly notice a reason not to buy. Marketers should always be on the look out for such barriers. This is one of the reasons that differentiation needs to be approached with caution: being different and appealing to one group in the market can turn consumers away.

A final word on how to grow

There are only a few key strategies to grow a brand. You can lower the price (and sacrifice profit margins), but this is self-defeating because a brand needs to grow to improve sales revenue and margins. You can improve the quality of the product or service for the same price, but this also negatively affects profit margins. Essentially, these two strategies are similar and not attractive. Everyday brand managers are trying to reduce costs and improve quality to stay competitive—usually that's about as far as you want to go with this strategy.

The other way to grow a brand is to invest in market-based assets—to improve the brand's mental and physical availability. However, just spending more on advertising will have similar results to the strategy above; it will cut your profits and there may be little to show for it afterwards. The trick is to make an investment that builds the brand's assets, so that in future the marketing budget gets a greater return. Building a distinctive memory structure achieves this; it enhances all future advertising (remember it is much easier to refresh existing memories, so advertising for brands that have distinctive elements embedded in people's minds suffers less from brand ambiguity). Obtaining new physical distribution has a very similar effect; again advertising and other marketing efforts work better if a brand is more widely available.

---

21 Think about the memory structures that this builds (e.g. 'I don't buy this brand!').

The third option to stimulate a brand's growth is to innovate and bring new or improved, desirable features to the marketplace. However, such advantages seldom last long, so it is important to 'make hay while the sun shines' and work fast to use the advantage to build penetration and enhance the brand's market-based assets. New or improved features are something to talk about; they attract attention and generate publicity. Unfortunately, a lot of 'innovation' is not exciting or newsworthy, and it is also very risky.

There is no magic key to growth. It's difficult because the potential returns are great and all your competitors are trying to grow too (at your brand's expense). But you are much more likely to succeed when it's understood that the key objective is to build its market-based assets. The brand must be easier to buy for more people in more situations. Market penetration is a good proxy measure for these assets, and so worth monitoring as a key metric. It's better than overall sales, because sales can be distorted by price promotions and other efforts that target your heavier, existing consumers.

Growth is possible—all the laws of marketing in this book support this—and it doesn't just depend on new products. Better advertising, better branding, better media strategy, better in-store displays and following the seven rules presented above—these are all paths to growth.

A FINE FUTURE FOR MARKETING

Few marketing departments see themselves as custodians of the precious market-based assets of mental availability (brand salience) and physical availability—at least not yet. While it is commonplace to talk about building strong brands (rather than short-run sales), brand managers have little specialist knowledge about building and managing these assets, and rarely if ever do they have comprehensive metrics covering mental and physical availability. Their efforts are seldom judged against such metrics. Considerable time is wasted on esoteric quackery concerned with segmentation, differentiation and how buyers perceive brands (e.g. brand personality).

However, as more brand managers realise how brands really compete, their attention should turn towards activities that build mental and physical availability. Their attention will then shift to branding, media strategy and distribution—there is a great deal of research, development and experimentation that needs to be done in these areas to improve marketing effectiveness.

Marketing today largely functions as a specialist part of the production department; it produces advertising and promotions rather than experimenting and learning about strategy. Development of specialist knowledge of these market-based assets should lead to greater respect for marketing as a crucial function of business. It is a significant opportunity because no other part of the organisation measures and therefore can claim to manage these intangible assets. The same cannot be said for other areas of a business, such as product development, customer service and pricing.

The future for marketing departments and for consumer brands is bright—if they adapt to the more complex and media-fragmented world we live in; if they become sophisticated mass marketers working with the empirical laws of marketing; and if they reject 'anything goes' lawless marketing strategy.

13

A Final Word

Byron Sharp

One thing that emerges from the law-like patterns discussed in this book is that *everything varies together*. As brands get bigger (i.e. gain market share) their metrics move in the opposite direction to the metrics of brands that are shrinking. Bigger brands have higher penetration and loyalty metrics (both attitudinal and behavioural). This pattern doesn't fit with many old theories of how markets work. But this is the way the real world works. This suggests that marketing metrics, including market share, all reflect one thing: popularity. Therefore, brands vary in their popularity, and everything flows from that. Also, two rival brands with similar levels of popularity will have very similar metrics.

These patterns are so robust that a single mathematical model predicts many of the laws in this book. This model is the NBD-Dirichlet model of brand choice and purchase rates (usually simply called 'the Dirichlet') (see Ehrenberg, Uncles & Goodhardt, 2004; Goodhardt, Ehrenberg & Chatfield, 1984). It is a model about consumers/buyers. It assumes that buying behaviour is heterogeneous and probabilistic; in other words, we each have a certain propensity to buy (some of us buy more often than others) and a certain propensity to buy particular brands (we each have our own preferences or personal repertoires). The Dirichlet is 25 years old and has survived 25 years of testing. It is one of marketing science's greatest achievements; for more information, see <www.MarketingScience.info>.

LAWS INTRODUCED IN THIS BOOK

- **Double jeopardy law**: Brands with less market share have so because they have far fewer buyers, and these buyers are slightly less loyal (in their buying and attitudes). See Chapter 2.

- **Retention double jeopardy**: All brands lose some buyers; this loss is proportionate with their market share, i.e. big brands lose more customers (though these lost customers represent a smaller proportion of their total customer base). See Chapter 3.

- **Pareto law, 60/20**: Slightly more than half of a brand's sales come from the top 20% of the brand's customers. The rest of the sales come from the bottom 80% of customers (i.e. the Pareto law is not 80/20). See Chapter 4.

- **Law of buyer moderation**: In subsequent time periods heavy buyers buy less often than in the base period that was used to categorise them as heavy buyers. Also, light buyers buy more often and some non-buyers become buyers. This regression to the mean phenomenon occurs even when there is no real change in buyer behaviour. See Chapter 4.

- **Natural monopoly law**: Brands with more market share attract a greater proportion of light category buyers. See Chapter 7.

- **User bases seldom vary**: Rival brands sell to very similar customer bases. See Chapter 5.

- **Attitudes and brand beliefs reflect behavioural loyalty**: Consumers know and say more about brands they use more often, and they think and say little about brands they do not use. Therefore, because they have more users, larger brands always score higher in surveys that assess buyers' attitudes to brands.

- **Usage drives attitude** (or I love my Mum, and you love yours): The attitudes and perceptions (about a brand) that a brand's customers express are very similar to the attitudes and perceptions expressed by customers of other brands (about their brand). See Chapter 5.

- **Law of prototypicality**: Image attributes that describe the product category score higher (i.e. are more commonly associated) than less prototypical attributes. See Chapter 8.

- **Duplication of purchase law**: A brand's customer base overlaps with the customer base of other brands, in line with their market share (i.e. a brand shares the most customers with large brands and the least number of customers with small brands). If 30% of a brand's buyers also bought brand A in a period, then 30% of every rival brand's customers also bought brand A. See Chapter 6.

- **NBD-Dirichlet**: A mathematical model of how buyers vary in their purchase propensities (i.e. how often they buy from a category and which brands they buy). This model correctly describes and explains many of the above laws. The Dirichlet is one of marketing's few true scientific theories.

Bibliography

Aaker, D 2001, *Strategic Market Management*, John Wiley & Sons, New York.

Aaker, J 1997, 'Dimensions of brand personality', *Journal of Marketing Research*, vol. 34, 347–56.

Alpert, M 1971, 'Identification of determinant attributes: a comparison of methods', *Journal of Marketing Research*, vol. 8, pp. 184–91.

Anschuetz, N 2002, 'Why a brand's most valuable customer is the next one it adds', *Journal of Advertising Research*, vol. 42, pp. 15–21.

Armstrong, J & Collopy, F 1996, 'Competitor orientation: effects of objectives and information on managerial decisions and profitability', *Journal of Marketing Research*, vol. 33 (May), pp. 188–99.

Armstrong, J & Schultz, R 1992, 'Principles involving marketing policies: an empirical assessment', *Marketing Letters*, vol. 4, no. 3, pp. 253–65.

Baldinger, A, Blair, E & Echambadi, R 2002, 'Why brands grow', *Journal of Advertising Research*, pp. 7–14.

Barnard, N & Ehrenberg, A 1990, 'Robust measures of consumer brand beliefs', *Journal of Marketing Research*, vol. 27, pp. 477–84.

Bass, F 1993, 'The future of research in marketing: marketing science', *Journal of Marketing Research*, 30th anniversary guest editorial, vol. 30, pp. 1–6.

Belch, G & Belch, M 2008, *Advertising and Promotion*, McGraw Hill, Melbourne.

Bellizzi, J, Crowley, A & Hasty, R 1983, 'The effects of color in store design', *Journal of Retailing*, vol. 59 (Spring), pp. 21–45.

Bennett, D 2005, 'What car will they buy next?', report 19 for corporate members, Ehrenberg-Bass Institute for Marketing Science, Adelaide.

Berger, J & Fitzsimons, G 2008, 'Dogs on the street, pumas on your feet: how cues in the environment influence product evaluation and choice,' *Journal of Marketing Research*, vol. 45 (February), pp. 1–14.

Bijmolt, T, van Heerde, H & Pieters, R 2005, 'New empirical generalization on the determinants of price elasticity', *Journal of Marketing Research*, vol. XLII (May), pp. 141–56.

Binet, L & Field, P 2007, *Marketing in the Era of Accountability*, World Advertising Research Centre, available from <www.warc.com>.

Bogomolova, S & Romaniuk, D 2005, 'Why do they leave? An examination of the reasons for customer defection in the business banking industry', Australia and New Zealand Marketing Academy Conference, Perth.

Broadbent, S 1989, *The Advertising Budget: The Advertiser's Guide to Budget Determination*, NTC Publications Ltd for Institute of Practitioners in Advertising, Henley-on-Thames, Oxon, United Kingdom.

Brodie, R, Bonfrer, A & Cutler, J 1996, 'Do managers overreact to each others' promotional activity? Further empirical evidence', *International Journal of Research in Marketing*, vol. 13, no. 4 (October), pp. 379–87.

Bullmore, J 1999, 'Advertising and its audience: a game of two halves', *International Journal of Advertising*, vol. 18, pp. 275–90.

Carpenter, G, Glazer, R & Nakamoto, K 1994, 'Meaningful brands from meaningless differentiation: the dependence on irrelevant attributes', *Journal of Marketing Research*, vol. 31, pp. 339–50.

Castleberry, S, Barnard, N, Barwise, T, Ehrenberg, A & Dall'Olmo Riley, F 1994, 'Individual attitude variations over time', *Journal of Marketing Management*, vol. 10, pp. 153–62.

Collins, M 2002, 'Analyzing brand image data', *Marketing Research*, vol. 14, pp. 33–6.

Colombo, R, Ehrenberg, A & Sabavala, D 2000, 'Diversity in analyzing brand-switching tables: the car challenge', *Canadian Journal of Marketing Research*, vol. 19, pp. 23–36.

Dall'Olmo Riley, F, Ehrenberg, A, Castleberry, S, Barwise, T & Barnard, N 1997, 'The variability of attitudinal repeat-rates', *International Journal of Research in Marketing*, vol. 14, pp. 437–50.

Danaher, P, Bonfrer, A & Dhar, S 2008, 'The effect of competitive advertising interference on sales of packaged goods', *Journal of Marketing Research*, vol. 45, pp. 211–25.

Danaher, P & Brodie, R 2000, 'Understanding the characteristics of price elasticities for frequently purchased packaged goods', *Journal of Marketing Management*, vol. 16, pp. 917–36.

Davidson, J 1976, 'Why most new consumer brands fail', *Harvard Business Review*, March/April, pp. 117–22.

Dickson, P & Sawyer, A 1990, 'The price knowledge and search of supermarket shoppers', *Journal of Marketing*, vol. 54 (July), pp. 42–53.

Dolnicar, S & Rossiter, J 2008, 'The low stability of brand-attitude associations is partly due to market research methodology', *International Journal of Research in Marketing*, vol. 21, pp. 104–8.

Drexler, K 1987, *Engines of Creation: The Coming Era of Nanotechnology*, Bantam, New York.

Driesener, C & Romaniuk, J 2006, 'Comparing methods of brand image measurement', *International Journal of Market Research*, vol. 48, pp. 681–98.

du Plessis, E 1994, 'Recognition versus recall', *Journal of Advertising Research*, vol. 34, no. 3, May/June, pp. 75–91.

du Plessis, E 2005, *The Advertised Mind: Ground-breaking Insights into How Our Brains Respond to Advertising*, Milward Brown and Kogan Page Limited, London.

East, R & Hammond, K 2005, 'Good news about bad news: talking about word of mouth', report 34 for corporate members, Ehrenberg-Bass Institute for Marketing Science, Adelaide.

Ehrenberg, A 1959, 'The pattern of consumer purchases', *Applied Statistics*, vol. 8, no. 1, pp. 26–41.

Ehrenberg, A 1993, 'Even the social sciences have laws', *Nature*, vol. 365, p. 385.

Ehrenberg, A 1998, 'Making data user-friendly', report 21 for corporate members, Ehrenberg-Bass Institute for Marketing Science, Adelaide.

Ehrenberg, A 1999, 'What we can and cannot get from graphs, and why', *Journal of Targeting, Measurement & Analysis for Marketing*, vol. 8, no. 2, pp. 113–34.

Ehrenberg, A 2000, 'Data reduction: analysing and interpreting statistical data', *Journal of Empirical Generalisations in Marketing Science*, vol. 5, available at <www.EmpGens.com>.

Ehrenberg, A 2004, 'My research in marketing: how it happened', *Marketing Research*, vol. 16, pp. 36–41.

Ehrenberg, A, Barnard, N & Scriven, J 1997, 'Differentiation or salience', *Journal of Advertising Research*, vol. 37, pp. 7–14.

Ehrenberg, A & Bound, J 1999, 'Customer retention and switching in the car market', report 6 for corporate members, Ehrenberg-Bass Institute for Marketing Science, Adelaide.

Ehrenberg, A, Hammond, K & Goodhardt, G 1994, 'The after-effects of price-related consumer promotions', *Journal of Advertising Research*, vol. 34, pp. 11–21.

Ehrenberg, A, Uncles, M & Goodhardt, G 2004, 'Understanding brand performance measures: using Dirichlet benchmarks', *Journal of Business Research*, vol. 57, pp. 1307–25.

Esslemont, D & Wright, M 1994, 'Essentialism: an unrecognised problem for marketers', *NZ Marketing Educators' Conference*, pp. 240–2.

Evans, F 1959, 'Psychological and objective factors in the prediction of brand choice Ford versus Chevrolet', *The Journal of Business*, vol. 32, pp. 340–69.

Fishbein, M & Ajzen, I 1975, *Belief, Attitude, Intention and Behaviour: An Introduction to Theory and Research*, Addison-Wesley Publishing Company, Reading, MA.

Flaherty, B 2007, 'Project Apollo and ad impact: improving returns from media expenditures', in ESOMAR, Dublin, pp. 444–53.

Fournier, S & Yao, J 1997, 'Reviving brand loyalty: a reconceptualization within the framework of consumer-brand relationships', *International Journal of Research in Marketing*, vol. 14, no. 5, pp. 451–72.

Gaillard, E & Romaniuk, J 2007, 'The uniqueness of brands', report 40 for corporate members, Ehrenberg-Bass Institute for Marketing Science, Adelaide.

Gaillard, E, Romaniuk, J & Sharp, A 2005, 'Exploring consumer perceptions of visual distinctiveness', in Australia and New Zealand Marketing Academy Conference, 5–7 December 2005, University of Western Australia, Fremantle.

Goodhardt, G, Ehrenberg, A & Chatfield, C 1984, 'The Dirichlet: a comprehensive model of buying behaviour', *Journal of the Royal Statistical Society*, vol. 147, no. 5, pp. 621–55.

Green, P, Goldberg, S & Montemayor, M 1981, 'A hybrid utility estimation model for conjoint analysis', *Journal of Marketing*, vol. 45, pp. 33–41.

Grimes, A & Doole, I 1998, 'Exploring the relationship between colour and international branding: a cross cultural comparison of the UK and Taiwan', *Journal of Marketing Management*, vol. 14, pp. 799–817.

Hall, D & Stamp, J 2004, *Meaningful Marketing: 100 Data-proven Truths and 402 Practical Ideas for Selling More with Less Effort*, Brain Brew Books, Ohio.

Hamilton, W, East, R & Kalafatis, S 1997, 'The measurement and utility of brand price elasticities', *Journal of Marketing Management*, vol. 13, no. 4, pp. 285–98.

Hammond, K, Ehrenberg, A & Goodhardt, G 1996, 'Market segmentation for competitive brands', *European Journal of Marketing*, vol. 30, pp. 39–49.

Hardie, B, Johnson, E & Fader, P 1993, 'Modeling loss aversion and reference dependence effects on brand choice', *Marketing Science*, vol. 12, no. 4 (Fall), pp. 378–94.

Hasher, L & Zacks, R 1984, 'Automatic processing of fundamental information: the case of frequency of occurrence', *American Psychologist*, vol. 39, pp. 1372–88.

Heath, R 2001, 'The hidden power of advertising: how low involvement processing influences the way we choose brands', *Admap*.

Heil, O & Helsen, K 2001, 'Toward an understanding of price wars: their nature and how they erupt', *International Journal of Research in Marketing*, vol. 18, pp. 83–98.

Hu, Y, Lodish, L, Krieger, A & Hayati, B 2009, 'An analysis of real world TV advertising tests: a recent update', *Journal of Advertising Research*, vol. 49, pp. 201–6.

Hunt, S & Morgan, R 1995, 'The comparative advantage theory of competition', *Journal of Marketing*, vol. 59, pp. 1–15.

Johnson, E 1997, 'The meaning of color in trademarks', The Annual Conference of the International Literacy Association, Wyoming.

Jones, J 1995a, 'Single-source research begins to fulfill its promise', *Journal of Advertising Research*, vol. 35, pp. 9–16.

Jones, J 1995b, *When Ads Work: New Proof that Advertising Triggers Sales*, Lexington Books, New York.

Jones, J 1997, 'Is advertising still salesmanship?', *Journal of Advertising Research*, pp. 9–15.

Juster, F 1960, 'Prediction and consumer buying intentions', *American Economic Review*, vol. 50, pp. 604–22.

Kahneman, D & Tversky, A 1979, 'Prospect theory: an analysis of decision under risk', *Econometrica*, vol. 47, no. 2, pp. 263–91.

Kahney, L 2004, *The Cult of Mac*, No Starch Press, San Fransisco.

Kamakura, W & Russell, G 1989, 'A probabilistic choice model for market segmentation and elasticity structure', *Journal of Marketing Research*, vol. 26, pp. 379–90.

Kay, J 1993, *Foundations of Corporate Success: How Business Strategies Add Value*, Oxford University Press, Oxford.

Kennedy, R & Ehrenberg, A 2000, 'Brand user profiles seldom differ', report 7 for corporate members, Ehrenberg-Bass Institute for Marketing Science, Adelaide.

Kennedy, R & Ehrenberg, A 2001a, 'Competing retailers generally have the same sorts of shoppers', *Journal of Marketing Communications*, vol. 7, pp. 1–8.

Kennedy, R & Ehrenberg, A 2001b, 'There is no brand segmentation', *Marketing Insights, Marketing Research*, vol. 13, no. 1, pp. 4–7.

Kennedy, R, Ehrenberg, A & Long, S 2000, 'Competitive brands' user-profiles hardly differ', Market Research Society Conference, Brighton, UK.

Kennedy, R, McDonald, C & Sharp, B 2008, 'Pure single source data and take off time for Project Apollo', *Admap*, pp. 32–5.

Klotz, I 1996, 'Bending perception: a book review', *Nature*, vol. 379, no. 1, p. 412.

Koch, R 1999, *The 80/20 Principle: The Secret to Success by Achieving More with Less*, Doubleday, New York.

Kotler, P 1992, 'Marketing's new paradigm: what's really happening out there', *Planning Review*, special issue, no. 20 (September/October), pp. 50–2.

Kotler, P 1994, *Marketing Management: Analysis, Planning, Implementation, and Control*, Prentice Hall, Englewood Cliffs, New Jersey.

Kotler, P, Armstrong, G, Brown, L & Adam, S 1998, *Marketing*, Prentice Hall, Sydney.

Lambert-Pandraud, R, Laurent, G & Lapersonne, E 2005, 'Repeat purchasing of new automobiles by older consumers: empirical evidence and inter-pretations', *Journal of Marketing*, vol. 69, pp. 97–113.

Lapersonne, E, Laurent, G & Le Goff, J 1995, 'Consideration sets of size one: an empirical investigation of automobile purchases', *International Journal of Research in Marketing*, vol. 12, pp. 55–66.

Lattin, J & Bucklin, R 1989, 'Reference effects of price and promotion on brand choice behavior', *Journal of Marketing Research*, vol. 26 (August), pp. 299–310.

Leenheer, J, Van Heerde, H, Bijmolt, T & Smidts, A 2007, 'Do loyalty programs really enhance behavioral loyalty? An emperical analysis accounting for self-selecting members', *International Journal of Research in Marketing*, vol. 24, pp. 31–47.

Lees, G, Garland, R & Wright, M 2007, 'Switching banks: old bank gone but not forgotten', *Journal of Financial Services Marketing*, vol. 12, pp. 146–56.

Liu, Y 2007, 'The long-term impact of loyalty programs on consumer purchase behavior and loyalty', *Journal of Marketing*, vol. 71, pp. 19–35.

Lodish, L, Abraham, M, Kalmenson, S, Livelsberger, J, Lubetkin, B, Richardson, B & Stevens, M 1995, 'How TV advertising works: a meta-analysis of 389 real world split cable TV advertising experiments', *Journal of Marketing Research*, vol. 32, pp. 125–39.

McClure, S, Li, J, Tomlin, D, Cypert, K, Montague, L & Montague, P 2004, 'Neural correlates of behavioral preference for culturally familiar drinks', *Neuron*, vol. 44, pp. 379–87.

McDonald, C 1969, 'Relationships between advertising exposure and purchasing behaviour', Market Research Society Conference.

McDonald, C & Ehrenberg, A 2003, 'What happens when brands gain or lose share? Customer acquisition or increased loyalty?', report 31 for corporate members, Ehrenberg-Bass Institute for Marketing Science, Adelaide.

McDonald, C & Sharp, B 2005, 'Individual-level advertising effects', report 36 for corporate members, Ehrenberg-Bass Institute for Marketing Science, Adelaide.

Mace, S & Neslin, S 2004, 'The determinants of pre- and post-promotion dips in sales of frequently purchased goods', *Journal of Marketing Research*, vol. 31 (August), pp. 339–50.

Mela, C, Gupta, S & Lehmann, D 1997, 'The long-term impact of promotion and advertising on consumer brand choice', *Journal of Marketing Research*, vol. 34 (May), pp. 248–61.

Mela, C, Jedidi, K & Bowman, D 1998, 'The long-term impact of promotions on consumer stockpiling behavior', *Journal of Marketing Research*, vol. 35 (May), pp. 250–62.

Meyer-Waarden, L & Benavent, C 2006, 'The impact of loyalty programmes on repeat purchase behaviour', *Journal of Marketing Management*, vol. 22, pp. 61–88.

Mills, K 2000, 'The form that TV ads take', report 10 for corporate members, Ehrenberg-Bass Institute for Marketing Science, Adelaide.

Morgan, R, Appiah-Adu, K & Ling, C 1995, 'Consumers' emotional response patterns to advertising stimuli', *Journal of Marketing Communications*, vol. 1, pp. 37–53.

Mullman, J 2007, 'Miller repeals "man law" ', *Advertising Age*, 22 January.

Mundt, K, Dawes, J & Sharp, B 2006, 'Can a brand outperform competitors on cross-category loyalty? An examination of cross-selling metrics in two financial services markets', *Journal of Consumer Marketing*, vol. 23, pp. 465–569.

Narasimhan, C, Neslin, S & Sen, S 1996, 'Promotional elasticities and category characteristics', *Journal of Marketing*, vol. 60 (April), pp. 17–30.

Nelson, P 1974, 'Advertising as information', *Journal of Political Economy*, vol. 82, pp. 729–54.

Parker, K & Stuart, T 1997, 'The West Ham syndrome', *International Journal of Market Research*, vol. 39, pp. 509–17.

Pauwels, K, Hanssens, D & Siddarth, S 2002, 'The long-term effects of price promotions on category incidence, brand choice, and purchase quantity', *Journal of Marketing Research*, vol. 39 (November), pp. 421–39.

Pauwels, K, Silva-Risso, J, Srinivasan, S & Hanssens, D 2004, 'New products, sales promotions, and firm value: the case of the automobile industry', *Journal of Marketing*, vol. 68 (October), pp. 142–56.

Popper, K 1976, *Unended Quest: An Intellectual Autobiography*, Fontana, London.

Redfern, C 2002, 'Not for girls? The yorkie and echo adverts', <www.thefword. org.uk>, accessed 2007.

Reeves, R 1961, *Reality in Advertising*, Knopf, New York.

Reichheld, F & Sasser, W 1990, 'Zero defections: quality comes to services', *Harvard Business Review*, vol. 68, pp. 105–11.

Riebe, E 2003, 'Normal rates of defection and acquisition and their relationship to market share change', PhD, University of South Australia, Adelaide.

Roberts, A 1994, 'Measuring advertising effects through panel data', European Advertising Effectiveness Symposium, June 9–10, Brussels.

Roberts, A 1996, 'What do we know about advertising's short-term effects?', *Admap*, pp. 42–5.

Roberts, A 1998, 'Measuring the short-term sales effects of TV advertising', *Admap*, pp. 50–6.

Roberts, K 2004, *Lovemarks: The Future beyond Brands*, Murdoch Books, Sydney.

Robinson, T, Borzekowski, D, Matheson, D & Kraemer, H 2007, 'Effects of fast food branding on young children's taste preferences', *Pediatrics and Adolescent Medicine*, vol. 161, pp. 792–7.

Romaniuk, J & Bogomolova, S 2005, 'Variation in brand trust scores', *Journal of Targeting, Measurement and Analysis for Marketing*, vol. 13, pp. 363–73.

Romaniuk, J & Sharp, B 2000, 'Using known patterns in image data to determine brand positioning', *International Journal of Market Research*, vol. 42, pp. 219–30.

Romaniuk, J & Sharp, B 2004a, 'Brand salience: what is it and why it matters', report 16 for corporate members, Ehrenberg-Bass Institute for Marketing Science, Adelaide.

Romaniuk, J & Sharp, B 2004b, 'Conceptualizing and measuring brand salience', *Marketing Theory*, vol. 4, no. 4, pp. 327–42.

Romaniuk, J, Sharp, B & Ehrenberg, A 2007, 'Evidence concerning the importance of perceived brand differentiation', *Australasian Marketing Journal*, vol. 15, pp. 42–54.

Rungie, C, Laurent, G, Dall'Olmo Riley, F, Morrison, D & Roy, T 2005, 'Measuring and modeling the (limited) reliability of free choice attitude questions', *International Journal of Research in Marketing*, vol. 22, pp. 309–18.

Schmittlein, D, Cooper, L & Morrison, D 1993, 'Truth in concentration in the land of (80/20) laws', *Marketing Science*, vol. 12, pp. 167–83.

Scriven, J & Ehrenberg, A 2004, 'Consistent consumer responses to price changes', *Australasian Marketing Journal*, vol. 12, no. 3, pp. 21–39.

Sharp, A 2002, 'Searching for boundary conditions for an empirical generalisation concerning the temporal stability of individual's perceptual responses', Doctor of Philosophy thesis, University of South Australia, Adelaide.

Sharp, A & Romaniuk, J 2002, 'Brand to attribute or attribute to brand: which is the path to stability?', European Marketing Academy 31st annual conference, 28–31 May, University of Minho, Portugal.

Sharp, A, Sharp, B & Redford, N 2003, 'Positioning and partitioning: A replication and extension', Australia and New Zealand Marketing Academy Conference, Adelaide.

Sharp, A & Winchester, M 2002, 'The temporal stability of negative brand image attributes', Australia and New Zealand Marketing Academy Conference, Melbourne.

Sharp, B 1995, 'Brand equity and market-based assets of professional service firms', *Journal of Professional Services Marketing*, vol. 13, pp. 3–13.

Sharp, B, Riebe, E, Dawes, J & Danenberg, N 2002, 'A marketing economy of scale: big brands lose less of their customer base than small brands', *Marketing Bulletin*, vol. 13, pp. 1–7.

Sharp, B & Romaniuk, J 2007, 'There is a Pareto Law but not as you know it', *Ehrenberg-Bass Institute Report for Corporate Sponsors*, No. 42.

Sharp, B & Sharp, A 1997a, 'Loyalty programs and their impact on repeat-purchase loyalty patterns', *International Journal of Research in Marketing*, vol. 14, pp. 473–86.

Sharp, B & Sharp, A 1997b, 'Positioning and partitioning', 26th European Marketing Academy Conference, 20–23 May, Warwick Business School, the University of Warwick, UK.

Sharp, B, Tolo, M & Giannopoulos, A 2001, 'A differentiatied brand should appeal to a special segment of the market … but it doesn't!', Australian and New Zealand Marketing Academy Conference: Bridging Marketing Theory & Practice, Massey University, Albany, New Zealand.

Simon, HA 1957, *Models of Man: Social and Rational*, Wiley, New York.

Singh, J, Ehrenberg, A & Goodhardt, G 2008, 'Measuring consumer loyalty to product variants', *International Journal of Market Research*, vol. 50, pp. 513–32.

Singh, J, Goodhardt, G & Ehrenberg, A 2001, 'Loyalty to product attributes', report 11 for corporate members, Ehrenberg-Bass Institute for Marketing Science, Adelaide.

Spaeth, J & Hess, M 1989, 'Single-source data … the missing pieces', published in the Proceedings of ARF Single-Source Data Workshop, 22 June.

Srivastava, R, Shervani, T & Fahey, L 1998, 'Market-based assets and shareholder value: a framework for analysis', *Journal of Marketing*, vol. 62, pp. 2–18.

Starr, D 1998, *Blood: An Epic History of Medicine and Commerce*, HarperCollins, New York.

Steenkamp, J, Nijs, V, Hanssens, D & Dekimpe, M 2005, 'Competitive reactions to advertising and promotion attacks', *Marketing Science*, vol. 24, no. 1, pp. 35–54.

Stern, P & Ehrenberg, A 2003, 'Expectations vs reality', *Marketing Insights*, *Marketing Research*, spring, pp. 40–3.

Swinyard, W 1995, 'The hard core and zen riders of Harley Davidson: a market-driven segmentation analysis', *Journal of Targeting, Measurement and Analysis for Marketing*, vol. 4, pp. 337–62.

Tellis, G 1988, 'The price elasticity of selective demand: a meta analysis of econometric models of sales', *Journal of Marketing Research*, vol. 25 (November), pp. 331–41.

Tellis, G 2009, 'Generalizations about advertising effectiveness in markets', *Journal of Advertising Research*, vol. 49, pp. 240–5.

Telser, L 1964, 'Advertising and competition', *Journal of Political Economy*, vol. 72, pp. 537–62.

Totten, J & Block, M 1994, *Analyzing Sales Promotions*, Dartnell Corporation, Chicago.

Trout, J & Rivkin, S 2000, *Differentiate or Die: Survival in Our Era of Killer Competition*, John Wiley & Sons, New York.

van Heerde, H, Leeflang, P & Wittink, D 2000, 'The estimation of pre- and post-promotion dips with store-level scanner data', *Journal of Marketing Research*, vol. 37 (August), pp. 383–95.

Vanhuele, M & Drèze, X 2002, 'Measuring the price knowledge shoppers bring to the store', *Journal of Marketing*, vol. 68 (October), pp. 72–85.

Verhoef, P 2003, 'Understanding the effect of customer relationship management efforts on customer retention and customer share development', *Journal of Marketing*, vol. 67, pp. 30–45.

Whitlark, D & Smith, S 2001, 'Using correspondence analysis to map relationships', *Marketing Research*, vol. 13, pp. 22–7.

Woodside, A & Waddle, G 1975, 'Sales effects of in-store advertising', *Journal of Advertising Research*, vol. 15, no. 3, pp. 29–33.